Nonviolence Daily

365 Days of Inspiration from Gandhi

MICHAEL N. NAGLER

STEPHANIE N. VAN HOOK

ISBN: 978-0-9978676-4-0

Library of Congress Control Number: 2019950599
The Metta Center for Nonviolence, founded in 1982, promotes the study and practice of nonviolence worldwide. Person Power Press, a project of the Metta Center for Nonviolence, publishes books on how to understand nonviolence and use it more safely and more effectively.
Learn about our work at www.mettacenter.org.

For more information about this book, please write to:
The Metta Center for Nonviolence
205 Keller Street, Suite 202 D
Petaluma, California 94952

Cover design: Miroslava Sobot, www.mika-art.com
Interior design: Kimberlyn David
Cover illustration: Sergio Garzon

Dedicated to everyone who has made nonviolence a central concern of their life,
and to everyone who ever will.

CONTENTS

INTRODUCTION

The characteristic of timeless wisdom is that it's, well, timeless.

Mahatma Gandhi has been called the most important human being of the twentieth century, and we think that's an understatement. You may come to agree with us as you read this book. Gandhi's seemingly endless creativity and equally endless energy resulted in him making original contributions in nearly every field of human activity, from healthcare and peace to education and democracy, not to mention economics.

Gandhi's contributions can be summed up as one all-important goal: to uplift the human image. His goal seems to have been to remind us of the unrealized, shining ideal in each and every one of us. So many of the urgent problems that beset us today can be traced to the lowering - or even the degradation - of the human image in our frantic, commercially driven and materialistically blinkered culture. Gandhi demonstrated through his own actions how each of us can bring our own positive capacities to life. Nonviolence was how he chose to express "insatiable love" for humankind. And the choice was wise.

We hope that we've succeeded to communicate something of that inspiring - and at the same time intensely pragmatic - spirit in the quotes we've chosen for comment in this book. Many of us grew up thinking Gandhi was unreachable, perched on an airy pedestal somewhere in a faraway land. For both of us, our eyes were opened to the timeless significance of Gandhi through the teachings of those who had seen and heard Gandhi firsthand. When the spirit of India had sunk to a low and seemingly irretrievable depth, they experienced the magic of Gandhi's uplifting genius.

As an early follower of Gandhi, Raihana Tyabji described the Mahatma's wisdom as such: "His consciousness took our consciousness and lifted it to unimaginable places."

The daily quotes curated for this book can be appreciated in various ways. They can, of course, be taken once a day, like a spiritual vitamin. They can be referred back to when specific problems arise, much in the way that Gandhi always referred to The Bhagavad Gita as his "spiritual reference book." You may wish to get together with friends and discuss what you find inspiring about the quotes. Those who are more interested in personal study will find ample space for taking notes on each page.

However you choose to engage with the book's material, it's a blessing for us to be on this journey with you. We both serve at the Metta Center for Nonviolence, where we say that true transformation - true revolution - is not about putting another person in power, but awakening a different power in people.

May these selections help us all wake up a little more together.

Stephanie N. Van Hook
Michael N. Nagler

KEY TERMS

You will come across several important terms throughout *Nonviolence Daily: 365 Days of Inspiration from Gandhi.* We explain those here, to galvanize your reading and your nonviolence practice.

Ahimsa: This ancient Sanskrit term usually translates as, and is possibly the model for, "nonviolence." The translation is unfortunate, however, in that such negative compounds in Sanskrit were more positive in effect than their corresponding, literal translations in English. For example, a*bhaya,* which literally means "non-fear," was actually the word for "courage." We spell "nonviolence" without a hyphen ("non-violence"), as doing so avoids emphasizing a negative - the mere absence of violence - when the word really stands for "love in action." It is likely that the word *himsa,* built on the Sanskrit root *√han* (strike, slay), was what linguists call a desiderative. So *ahimsa* should actually be translated as something like "the force unleashed when desire to harm is eradicated." Of course, "nonviolence" is handier! And that's fine, as long as we realize its limitations. See Nonviolence.

Ashram: Since time immemorial in India (with parallels in other monastic traditions), spiritual aspirants have gathered around a spiritual teacher in intentional communities to practice under ideal conditions (*a-shram* comes from a root meaning exertion). Gandhi founded four such communities throughout his career, and they served as training grounds for those who were preparing themselves for spiritually based activism. These intentional communities were also "home base" for activists during campaigns. When he began referring to these communities as "ashrams," upon his return to India in 1915, Gandhi was essentially acknowledging that he considered his activism to be spiritual in nature, rather than merely political.

The Bhagavad Gita: Gandhi called The Bhagavad Gita his "mother" and his "spiritual reference book." The Gita appears as a section of seven hundred verses within the ancient Indian epic the Mahabharata, where the warrior prince, Arjuna, collapses in dismay at the prospect of going into battle against his own relatives. He is admonished and encouraged by his charioteer Krishna (none other than an incarnation of Vishnu), and their exchange amounts to a discussion about the nature of human duty and what constitutes appropriate human action. As a warrior, Arjuna's duty is to fight, but he is reluctant for reasons of personal attachment: those he must kill are his relatives. Krishna's task is to lead Arjuna to understand that he must carry out his duty, setting aside even the most powerful of personal attachments. Gandhi explained that the story should not be taken literally. The Gita delivers a powerful message: To reach self-actualization, we must "kill" what we most cherish, our personal attachments. Ultimately, this means extinguishing the ego. The story of Arjuna on the battlefield represents the story of our own inner struggle to overcome selfish impulses like anger, fear, and greed. It is from this struggle that nonviolence springs.

Civil Disobedience: the deliberate, open violation of a law held to be unjust, along with the willing acceptance of the prescribed punishment for violating that law. Civil disobedience can also be referred to as "nonviolent direct action" when the action taken is considered to be illegal or challenges a law. "Civil resistance" is used interchangeably with civil disobedience by some who see a law as being in violation of a more fundamental "higher" law. Civil resistance is therefore not so much a matter of disobeying a law but of following a higher or more natural law. See Obstructive Program.

Constructive Program: This term was coined by Gandhi. It describes nonviolent action taken within a community to build structures, systems, processes, or resources that are positive alternatives to oppression. It can be seen as self-improvement of both community and individual. Constructive program often works alongside obstructive program, or civil disobedience, which usually involves direct confrontation to, or non-cooperation with, oppression. Constructive program is doing what one can to imaginatively and positively create justice within one's own community.

Dehumanization: seeing an individual or an entire group of people as lacking human qualities. Dehumanization occurs when people view others as inferior. While no one can clearly pinpoint all the reasons for violent action, most sociologists and historians believe that dehumanization is an antecedent to violence: humans do not persecute groups or individuals they perceive as equal. Dehumanization is therefore the first, crucial link in the long and barbarous chain of violent action that is overcome only through rehumanization, or the nonviolent process of rekindling empathy.

Heart Unity: Gandhi cherished unity at the heart, or spiritual level of being. He equally valued diversity on the surface level, in differences of race, gender, worldview - and even of status, wealth, and power. This valuation of surface diversity differentiates the spiritually based system of principled nonviolence from the more politically grounded approaches to justice, which try to reach unity by leveling surface differences. Practically speaking, one achieves heart unity with another when wishing fulfillment and happiness to the other, despite, or indeed partly because of, any surface differences. This state of mind rests on the belief that solutions to all problems exists, and that these solutions can meet the real needs, if not the conditioned wants, of all parties.

Mirror Neurons: The brain's mirror neurons fire not only when an animal acts, but also when an animal observes another animal act. Brain scientists at the University of Parma in Italy discovered these neurons in the late 1980s. The discovery was made using new, non-invasive technologies that enable scientists to detect the activity, or firing, of single neurons in brains, in this case the brains of monkeys. Mirror neurons have also been well documented in humans, leading one researcher, Marco Iacoboni of UCLA, to state that we are "wired for empathy," because our central nervous system is fine-tuned to mirror the intentions of others. If, as Gandhi insisted, nonviolence is a science, we have now opened a window onto its physiology - into our evolutionary inheritance of compassion.

Nonviolence: Gandhi called this force in human consciousness a "living power," and a scientist today would likely call it a form of "subtle energy." Nonviolence can be engaged, with suitable training, whether by individuals or groups, to effect positive changes on people and society, including epochal changes like dislodging a dictator or (as in India) ending a colonial era. This force relies upon the ultimate good in every human being, and therefore it affirms the humanity for everyone, even those whose behaviors have to be changed. Nonviolence is a science in the sense that its operations obey laws that can be discovered by study and practice, and science as we know it today has begun to verify its operations and presence throughout history, indeed throughout evolution. Gandhi did not hesitate to call nonviolence "the law of the humans."

Obstructive Program: Michael N. Nagler coined this term to define the use of civil disobedience to change an unjust or oppressive social order. Obstructive program, together with constructive program, make up the two branches of Gandhi's satyagraha.

Person Power: Michael N. Nagler invented this term to describe the core energy at the heart of any nonviolent social movement. Nonviolence begins when a person transforms fear, anger, or aggression into universal love, compassion, and resilience. Person power accounts for the fact that people power focuses on masses, overlooking the importance of the individual in revealing nonviolent truth. Both person power and people power contrast with, and often stand in opposition to, state power.

Satyagraha: Gandhi used the Sanskrit word *satyagraha,* or "clinging to truth," in reference to his campaigns in South Africa and India, such as the famous Salt March of 1930. Satyagraha can be understood as the vast inner strength or "soul force" required for nonviolent acts. As a spiritually based resistance, it starts in the heart and inevitably produces creative action. The term is used today to mean (1) the general principle of clinging to truth necessary for nonviolence work and (2) direct resistance through obstructive program and constructive program. Practitioners are known as *satyagrahis.*

NONVIOLENCE DAILY
365 DAYS OF INSPIRATION

DAY 1

Some Englishmen state that they took, and they hold,
India by the sword. Both these statements are wrong.
The sword is entirely useless for holding India.
We alone keep them.
– Gandhi, *Hind Swaraj*

The lie that violence projects is that it is all-powerful, and once someone uses it against us we are hopeless to overcome it. Gandhi realized that the spark of nonviolence resides in the reality that violence can really only work if we submit to it. For this reason, nonviolence requires an enormous faith in ourselves, though that faith alone is not enough. We need an alternative towards which we can turn, as Gandhi knew during the Indian Freedom Struggle. His style of empowerment: If you want nonviolence to be real, give people something concrete to do. Don't just make them dream about a better system, give them a way to participate in building it; let them strive to uphold it.

DAY 2

Differences of opinion should never mean hostility.
– Gandhi, *Young India,* March 1, 1927

Where there is more than one person, there will be differences of opinion. How we handle differences of opinion is a litmus test of our relationship to and comfort with conflict. Someone who is conflict-avoidant may avoid discussing differences of opinion in fear of upsetting the other person. Someone else may dive directly into those hard conversations with a sense that their opinion is the only valid one, and any difference of opinion a sign of an inexcusable ignorance rather than a healthy sign of differences in life experiences.

The more secure we are in our position, the less we feel shaken when someone disagrees with us, and the less we feel we need to defend it at all costs from those who think otherwise. A person trained in nonviolence will not passively avoid difficult conversations and differences of opinion when they matter, but will use discernment and self-restraint in deciding what is important to disagree about and when to keep quiet and wait it out.

A hostile attitude on our behalf might keep us from learning something new, or seeing another person in a new light. When we interrupt hostility within ourselves, we interrupt a cycle of violence. We can disagree and still maintain the dignity of the other person.

DAY 3

Bravery is not man's monopoly.
– Gandhi, *Harijan,* January 5, 1947

As the world's consciousness evolves to understand that all human beings are worthy of dignity, equality, economic justice, and respect, it is the realm of nonviolent action that portrays this reality most effectively.

Nonviolence is a humanizing force. One reaps the benefits of its power sometimes by participating in it and at other times witnessing it in action.

When we take time to witness nonviolence in action, we begin to take note that it's not something that only one group of people offer. We see it everywhere and in everyone at some level.

DAY 4

No one commits crime for the fun of it.
– Gandhi, *Harijan*, November 2, 1947

In order to inflict violence on someone, we must first dehumanize them. For this reason, Gandhi maintained that words like "crime" and "criminal" should be erased from our vocabulary. These words help us write off the dignity of the human being and dehumanize people before we subject them to our incarceration systems' psychological, and often physical, violence.

If someone has violated some part of our social contract, we must find a way to understand why. Was it an act of civil disobedience? Should we adjust the law? Is the person suffering from a trauma - and if so, what caused it in the first place, and what is being done to heal it? How can we apply what's called "restorative justice"?

Nonviolence is a force that heals. We must question any assumptions we or others might hold that people (or specific groups of people) want to do harm, and that the only way to "help" them is restraining or punishing them. We have to replace that violent worldview with the nonviolent vision that all people are human beings who are worthy of dignity, like ourselves.

DAY 5

There should be no mistake. There is no civil disobedience possible, until the crowds behave like disciplined soldiers.
– Gandhi, *Young India*, August, 25, 1921

Gandhi, to the surprise of many pacifists, participated indirectly in several war efforts, including Indian recruitment for World War I, feeling that since he had appealed to the Crown for redress at times, he had no right to abandon Britain at her hour of need. Through his experiences, he came to have a deep admiration for soldiers - not for the sanctioned murder they perform or the politics they espouse, but for the organization, discipline, restraint, and courage they must ideally cultivate. He dreamt of the power of an organized form of resistance as prepared, trained, and disciplined as an army, but based on nonviolence. Gandhi also had a strong sense that soldiers were the perfect audience for the message of nonviolence. To be nonviolent, we have to be courageous: we have to renounce the violence of which we know we are capable.

While running away from violence, or simply avoiding it, has no power, renouncing violence has power. Gandhi maintained that until the crowds could see themselves as disciplined soldiers - capable of violence, yet willing and able to restrain themselves from using it, and organized in a way that put their restraint and discipline on display - their civil disobedience wouldn't deploy its full power.

DAY 6

True economics is the economics of justice.
– Gandhi, *Sarvodaya*

Gandhi was confident in the power of new economic models. After reading John Ruskin's *Unto This Last* while in South Africa, Gandhi set up his first experiment in communal living, Phoenix Settlement. By sharing what we have, he realized, we minimize our needs and many of the injustices between us. He was convinced that economics could be the expression of our human goodness, our awareness of the whole of life, and our capacity to serve others. Such an economics boils down to three key principles. It embraces the duty of paying fair wages, because our personal wellbeing depends on the wellbeing of all. Competition would be based on the development of our skills, not on our willingness to work for less money than others because that's our only chance of getting work. And most importantly, we would view everything we have as a trust - nothing would be used or directed towards harming life.

DAY 7

I do not believe that an education of the heart can be imparted through books. It can only be done through the living touch of the teacher.
– Gandhi, *Young India,* September 1, 1921

Gandhi's vision of a new education, *nai talim,* aimed at the mind, body, and spirit - the integral development of the whole person.

Books alone cannot teach us how to be kind to others. We can read about lofty ideals in books, though we will find it difficult to carry out these ideals without the guidance of people who show us the way. Only other human beings can move us to forgive one another, teaching us by their own examples. Only other human beings can encourage us to work together harmoniously, again through their examples.

In the development of the new education movement within the Indian Freedom Struggle, Gandhi did not worry whether the teachers he sent from the movement to establish schools were literate or not. He looked instead for examples of inner character. Was this person patient and loving? He would send him. Was she determined and hard-working? He would send her. Gandhi demonstrated that the foundation for all intellectual knowledge rests upon the willingness to carry out the responsibility to take care of one another, a true education of the heart.

DAY 8

Happiness means an enlightened realization of human dignity and a craving for human liberty which prizes itself above mere selfish satisfaction of personal comforts and material wants and would readily and joyfully sacrifice these.
– Gandhi, *Young India,* March 5, 1931

One day, a reporter asked Gandhi what his secret was. Since Gandhi was observing his day of silence, he jotted his response on a piece of paper: "Renounce and enjoy." Gandhi knew much of the Upanishads by heart, including his favorite verse from the Isha, which he likely paraphrased in answering the reporter:

> The Lord is enshrined in the hearts of all. The Lord is the supreme reality. Rejoice in him through renunciation. Covet nothing. All belongs to the Lord. Thus working may you live a hundred years. Thus alone can you work in full freedom.

These words were integral to Gandhi's consciousness, forming his character and daily actions. For those of us inundated with commercial messages claiming that happiness comes from consuming, the message of the Isha - and of Gandhi - offers us an inviting challenge. He is saying: *Do you want to be really happy? Do you want to experience real freedom? Then offer someone dignity.*

DAY 9

The mere title of a doctor is no criterion;
a real doctor is he who is a true servant.
– Gandhi, *Harijan*, February 10, 1946

Dr. Izzeldin Abuelaish was born in the Jabalia refugee camp in the Gaza Strip, and he became the first Palestinian to work in an Israeli hospital. Tragically, in 2009, he lost his two daughters and niece when his home in Gaza was hit by a shell from an Israeli tank. He was devastated but not defeated. Instead of filling himself with hatred for Israelis, he decided to continue working for healing - by delivering Israeli and Palestinian babies into the world. Convinced that doctors can be messengers of peace, he has since dedicated his energies, passion, and grief into a force for change by empowering women's education in the Middle East through his foundation, Daughters for Life. Gandhi would say that Abuelaish is a real doctor: a true servant of nonviolence.

DAY 10

Love and exclusive possession can never go together. Theoretically, where there is perfect love, there is perfect non-possession.
– Gandhi, *Modern Review*, October 1935

Genuine love requires more than just refraining from hurting others. By developing our nonviolence, we work towards becoming love itself - serving and deeply nourishing those around us. We become a force for good.

How does one embody a perfect state of love, imperfect as we all are? Instead of grasping for what we see in front of us, be it a partner or a resource of some kind, we can detach ourselves from that something or someone. The space left where we were holding on is like a pocket of power, which when released becomes ours to direct towards our highest goals.

In the complexity of relationships with the people and things in our lives, the mind's natural tendency is to grasp onto these as "mine." We grow in our capacity to love by interrupting the possessive habit of mind. Gandhi is showing us with his life that this is true, and he is daring us to try it.

DAY 11

Satyagraha is gentle, it never wounds.
– Gandhi, *Harijan,* April 5, 1933

At what point do we lose our gentleness as grown-ups? We say a harsh word here, think a resentful thought there. It is not easy to be gentle, especially when others are not so gentle to us. But Gandhi reminds us that to use satyagraha, we need gentleness alongside an inner toughness. Indeed, the former requires the latter: without the tough "clinging to truth" that defines satyagraha, we are afraid to be gentle, mistakenly thinking it means to be vulnerable and weak. We therefore strive as nonviolent actors to be gentler with ourselves and others, and towards our planet.

DAY 12

Compassion or love is the human being's greatest excellence.
– Gandhi, *Indian Opinion*, August 9, 1913

We recommend memorizing the Prayer of St. Francis as a passage to guide us in the work of peacemaking:

> Lord, make me an instrument of thy peace: where there is hatred,
> let me sow love; where there is injury, pardon;
> where there is doubt, faith; where there is despair, hope;
> where there is darkness, light; where there is sadness, joy.
>
> O divine Master, grant that I may not so much seek to be consoled
> as to console,
> to be understood as to understand, to be loved as to love.
> For it is in giving that we receive,
> It is in pardoning that we are pardoned,
> And it is in dying to self that we are born to eternal life.

DAY 13

An awakened and intelligent public opinion is
the most potent weapon of a Satyagrahi.
– Gandhi, *Young India*, August 8, 1929

Gandhi felt that it was necessary in a nonviolent action to get the public to pay attention to what one is doing. His faith in human nature was such that when the public observed the dynamic of right against might, he believed they would be compelled to identify with the side speaking to the highest image of who we are. Once you have the public's attention and offer a dramatic example of nonviolence, rousing their opinion for your cause gets easier, and a tipping point occurs. If at that point someone (or someones) still wants to engage in the negative behavior which you have campaigned against, they are undoubtedly communicating that they are against the good of the community. It now becomes everyone's duty to non-cooperate with that person (or party) until they desist from their actions.

DAY 14

The law of love knows no bounds of space or time.
—Gandhi, *Young India,* January 8, 1925

Modern science is just catching up to the insights shared by the world's great mystics. In quantum physics, for instance, we have the theory of non-locality, demonstrating that a quantum event can occur in one region and affect another simultaneously. Einstein called it "spooky distance effects" (*Spukhafte fernwirkungen*). But there is nothing spooky about nonviolence!

If people in Ferguson, Missouri are inspired to follow the dedication of people halfway across the world in Gaza, that is the law of love traveling across the bounds of space. Even with the technologies that bind us, the only "technology" that can convince a people to take up nonviolence is the heart - the deep desire to make long-term change for the good of all. That desire does not have to touch us physically to move us. It simply arises and we can catch hold of, and direct it.

Similarly, nonviolence transcends the bounds of time. There will never be a time when we cannot draw from the legacies of the wise teachers of nonviolence. They have hit upon a bedrock of reality itself. We can read the words of those who have seen the power of nonviolence, contemplate their truth and relevance, and allow ourselves to be changed by them. We do not need to have Gandhi in front of us to learn from him; we only have to invite his timeless message into our hearts.

DAY 15

Life is but an endless series of experiments.
– Gandhi, *Young India*, September 25, 1924

When approaching life in the spirit of nonviolence, we must do so with humility. In striving and doing our level best, we move closer to becoming – and effecting – a positive force that generates healing, understanding, and reconciliation. On this path, we are experimenters in wisdom: we make a hypothesis, test it out, and refine it. Like the roots of a plant that will seek nourishment from where it exists in the soil, or turn its head to face the sun in whatever direction that may be, nonviolence tells us that if we have the daring, in whatever situation we find ourselves, we can change the direction of our life and try a new way.

DAY 16

Civilization, in the real sense of the term, consists not in the multiplication, but in the deliberate and voluntary reduction of wants.
– Gandhi, *The Mind of Mahatma Gandhi*

There is nothing wrong with having what we need to live well, and even thrive. Gandhi's concern is that consumerism, or the multiplication of our wants, only makes us more insecure and dependent on others. He wants to encourage us in every way possible to liberate ourselves from the false belief that we need to be fulfilled by consuming things, when what really makes us secure are deep, caring relationships.

The less we try to grasp onto things and people as though our sense of security depended on them, the greater will be our awareness of others' needs, along with the true nature of happiness. As the Buddha said, "no more sorrow will come, no more burden will fall" to those who do not try to possess things or people as their own. Simplicity in our thoughts, words, and deeds points the way forward in nonviolence.

DAY 17

A definite forgiveness would mean a definite recognition of our strength.
– Gandhi, *Mahatma, Vol. 2*

When it is not confronted with nonviolent resistance, violence can cause us to close down inside and carry hurts and burdens within ourselves, which when left unacknowledged and unaddressed, can lead to negative patterns in terms of how we see ourselves and our capacities. Forgiveness in its fullness is a means for stopping that truly vicious cycle.

Forgiveness is never an obligation. We sell forgiveness short in that it is rarely if ever presented in its true form as a gift and a choice. It is presented as a moral and religious imperative on the one hand, and as a sign of weakness on the other. Gandhi's view of forgiveness shines a bright light, allowing us to rediscover this incredible power.

When we do not forgive others, we carry resentment and fear in our hearts. Forgiveness shows us that there is a kind of strength that comes from acknowledging our humility and interdependence. Instead of fanning the flames of resentment in one another, we can model in our own lives that we desire to put an end to suffering and are willing to act on it.

DAY 18

Not knowing the stuff of which nonviolence is made, many have honestly believed that running away from danger every time was a virtue compared to offering resistance.
– Gandhi, *Harijan,* July 20, 1935

One of the most insidious misconceptions about nonviolence that pervades popular culture is that it means doing nothing at all. It is as though we think that the only alternative to violence is passive compliance. Not at all. We are talking about nonviolence, not non-action.

Even Gandhi dealt with this faulty assumption over and over again, yet he kept on addressing it in new ways. Anytime he wrote or spoke or offered resistance, he referred to nonviolence in all of its complexity. Here's a new assumption that we can embrace: nonviolence actually does work. It seems appropriate to riff off the Sufi poet Rumi: Between violence and passivity, there is a field. It's called nonviolence, and I'll meet you there.

DAY 19

Nonviolence should never be used as a shield for cowardice.
It is a weapon of the brave.
– Gandhi, *Mahatma, Vol. 7*

In his book *Courage in Both Hands*, the late Quaker activist Allan A. Hunter tells the story of Mrs. Pean-Pages, headmistress of a girls' school in Paris during World War II. Mrs. Pean-Pages had been hiding twenty-five girls, and one day a Gestapo officer came to her door saying he had a list of the girls' names and demanding that she hand them over. What you would you have done? Would you have lied? Would you have given up all hope?

Mrs. Pean-Pages did neither, which took immense courage and faith. She recalls first of all praying ("What can I do to maintain my values in this hopeless situation?"). She knew that the officer was not lying to her - he did have their names. So she decided to do something counterintuitive to her fear: She admitted that it was true, that she was hiding twenty-five children. "But," she added with marked anger in her voice (because you can be angry and nonviolent), "You knew for some time now that they were here and it is only now that you are coming to take them away. I will tell your superiors about this!" The officer confessed that she was right, and then did something amazing himself: He asked her not to tell anyone about it and turned away and left. No one returned for the girls. Mrs. Pean-Pages had saved the girls' lives through her audacious, nonviolent courage, and maybe, we can admit, the Gestapo officer also did his part.

DAY 20

We had lost the power of saying "no." It had become disloyal, almost sacrilegious to say "no" to the Government.
– Gandhi, *Young India,* June 1,1921

Our ability to say "no" to what we regard as wrong is as necessary to a democratic society as our ability to say "yes" to that which we approve and can accept. A nonviolent, and therefore democratic, society does not function on compulsion or coercion, but on freedom and persuasion, which rests on our ability to choose for ourselves.

Do we really possess the valuable capacity of choice today? When we go to the supermarket and find thousands of items to choose from, is that choice? Is it of deep consequence whether we buy this brand or that brand? There is an illusion of choice within the ideology of consumption, the untruth (and therefore, Gandhi would say, the violence) that we must buy something to be fulfilled.

Real choice means choosing between nonviolence and violence. The catch is this: Until we know what nonviolence is, we cannot choose it freely. Therefore, we must make every effort to learn more about nonviolence. It is not weakness or cowardice or even passivity. It is an active, regenerative, and truly democratic power that topples dictators and offers a sophisticated solution to the violent system from which we currently suffer.

DAY 21

"If you had hurt an Englishman," said Jan Smuts, "I would have shot you, even deported your people. As it is, I would have put you in prison and tried to subdue you and your people in every way. But how long can I go on like this when you do not retaliate?"
– Gandhi, *Harijan*, September 26, 1946

General Jan Smuts, Gandhi's considerable opponent in South Africa, spoke candidly about the way that the nonviolence of the Satyagraha struggle confounded and transformed him. In the quote above, Smuts gives insight into the mindset of a person who is defending a harmful system through the use of violent force: if someone from their side is harmed, they will use that as a justification for violence. But when nonviolence was offered, violence was much harder to justify.

The police force in America is an example of how this works. Hurt one of "theirs," and it's trouble for everyone - and it makes national news. But resist them nonviolently, and see what happens. As we learned from the 1960s Civil Rights struggle, the results of nonviolent resistance are amazing. Few still follow this method (so great is our need for movement discipline!). Effective nonviolent resistance, like that from the 1960s, is what Gandhi would call an appeal to the heart. The head would say, "Do to them what they did to you!" But nonviolence says, "Be more creative."

DAY 22

The practice of law ought not to mean taking more daily than, say, a village carpenter's wage.
– Gandhi, *Harijan,* July 13, 1940

Society teaches us that some work is "naturally" more important and more valuable than other kinds of work, and that some people are therefore worth more than other people. Who really benefits from the violence inherent in the perpetuation of class consciousness?

Early in his law career, at that teetering moment before he fully plunged himself into the path of public service and nonviolence, Gandhi thought that all work that contributed to society should be regarded as equal, from the farmer to the lawyer. At the same time, he confessed that he felt strongly that the work of the farmer was much more worthwhile than other professions. Why? Agriculture is precious, since it is related to human survival itself.

Gandhi realized that when farmers are exploited, we lose access to our most basic connection to the earth through our food systems, and everyone loses. Society can go on without the art of interpreting law, not without the sacred art of agriculture.

DAY 23

Satyagraha is a law of universal application. Beginning with the family, its use can be extended to every other circle.
– Gandhi, *Harijan,* March 31, 1946

The more we learn the skills of resisting those closest to us when we are called to do so, the stronger those skills are when we apply them to those from whom we have more detachment.

To use satyagraha in our homes means that we are never willing to inflict harm or punishment on those around us. When some children in Gandhi's ashram were caught "misbehaving," probably for some minor offense, he decided that instead of punishing them, he would fast (he believed that punishment had no place on an ashram).

On the one hand, if the ashram children were misbehaving, he was not free from blame; and secondly, by fasting, he could take on the suffering in the situation, giving the children an opportunity to recognize by his act their relationship to the rest of their community. When they had lost sight of their unity with the whole, the children were reminded of it through Gandhi's willingness to take on suffering in his own body, whereas punishment might have led them to rebel further.

DAY 24

I cannot impose my personal faith on others, never on a national organization. I can but try to convince the nation of its beauty and its usefulness.
– Gandhi, *Young India,* November, 20, 1924

Perhaps Antoine de Saint-Exupéry was influenced by Gandhi when he wrote: "If you want to build a ship, don't drum up people to collect wood and don't assign them tasks and work, but rather teach them to long for the endless immensity of the sea."

It's the same idea here. If you want to build a base of popular support for a movement, you don't need to give people pithy placards or weapons; you give them a mirror in which to see their own beauty and purpose. We have such a mirror, but it's often dusty. Nonviolence is what we use to wipe it clean.

To heed Gandhi's wisdom to meet this difficult task, we have to enlarge our view of what a human being is and what life is for. If we are here only to serve ourselves - if we have no ultimate responsibility to the planet, if other people are simply abstractions - then violence would make perfect sense. But who, having experienced a nonviolent moment, would actually maintain this? Life itself reveals itself when we align our thoughts, speech, and actions with its highest image.

DAY 25

My life has been an open book. I have no secrets
and I encourage no secrets.
– Gandhi, *Young India,* March 19, 1931

Gandhi never organized against his so-called opponents in secrecy. They were invited along in his thought process every inch of the way. When he set out on the famous Salt March, he telegrammed the names of all the marchers and their route to the Viceroy. This is what we call in nonviolence a "pull" model. Instead of pushing something onto others, for which they may or may not be ready psychologically or spiritually, we "pull" them along with us by the force of our example.

Gandhi points towards the liberation that comes from living life in the open - as well as the courage to do so. If we mire our lives in secrecy, we increase the potential for violence, including exploitation, extortion, and other forms of abuse. The more we take heart and move into the open with our personal and political struggles, the more power we can have.

DAY 26

The more we give up our attachment to the physical
frame of the person we love, the purer and more
expansive our love grows.
– Gandhi, *Day to Day with Gandhi, Vol. 1*

Another term for nonviolence is "love-in-action." It is not always an apt term, because what is *not* active about love? When seen in its true form, it is ever active, ever at work.

Love is both a precious and infinite resource. The more we love, the more we are able to love, and the deeper we can love others. While other people can teach us lessons about love, they are not its source. Love is its own source, and we are expressions of it.

The "purer and more expansive" our love becomes, the more powerful we become. When we resist, we do it in the name of love, not in the name of hatred. When we create, we create not for the few or even simply the majority, we build for everyone. That's love.

If we find ourselves attached to loving someone's physical frame, we can learn to love them more by attaching ourselves to what is within them that is in everyone. Our beloved comes alive in all, and so we will want to work for all. Doing so, we can find and experience love's highest fulfillment, which Hollywood can hardly dream of.

DAY 27

A small body of determined spirits fired by an unquenchable faith in their mission can alter the course of history.
– Gandhi, *Harijan, November 19, 1936*

Nonviolence is sometimes referred to as "people power." This is a perfectly valid idea, but we should not think of nonviolence solely as the power of large masses of people in a protest. There is another, possibly even more important, face of nonviolence: person power. With person power, it is not a question of numbers, however necessary they are in some situations, but a matter of individual commitment and ability to stay the nonviolent course.

When we possess determination, we will not let any of our seeming failures keep us from trying again. When we have an unquenchable faith in our mission, we will not accept anything less than its full realization - we will not be dissuaded from believing that a nonviolent future is possible. Whether we team up or go at it as individuals, we can alter the course of history, making the world safer and healthier for all who come after us.

DAY 28

The conviction has been growing upon me that things of fundamental importance to the people are not secured by reason alone, but have to be purchased with their suffering.
– Gandhi, *Young India,* March 19, 1931

When one undertakes nonviolent discipline, one is preparing to take on suffering - without offering it in return. The lunch-counter sit-ins in the American South illustrate how this discipline is very different from passively enduring violence. More than simply reasoning with people that lunch counters should be integrated, the sit-in activists committed to nonviolence, got trained by strategic movement thinkers, prepared for violent pushback, and sat down at those counters.

David Hartsough recalls a sit-in experience in his book *Waging Peace: Global Adventures of a Lifelong Activist.* At one lunch counter in Virginia, a man pulled David off his stool, held a knife to his throat, and told him to get out of there. Hartsough looked the man in the eye and said, "Brother, you do what you feel is right; and I will try to love you, anyway." The man's hand shook as he dropped his knife and walked out.

David's willingness to accept suffering was more powerful than the threat of violence. This is the kind of suffering to which Gandhi refers - not enduring injustice, but willingly taking on the suffering the situation may entail to transform it. By implication, he is telling us that we can hone this powerful capacity to even greater degrees.

DAY 29

My effort should never be to undermine another's faith, but to make him a better follower of his own faith.
– Gandhi, *Mahatma, Vol. 2*

Throughout Gandhi's life, many of his friends wanted to convert him to Christianity, thinking that Hinduism, his own religion, was inferior. Before he departed for England as a young man, Gandhi's mother gave him a necklace with religious significance reminding him of his devotion to her, as well as three vows she had asked him to take (no meat, no women, and no alcohol). His friend tried to get him to remove the necklace, calling it a superstition. He was also invited to join many Bible study meetings, which he attended out of curiosity and interest in the religion itself. Rather than convert to another faith, however, Gandhi decided to begin understanding his own at a deeper level, and he turned to the Bhagavad Gita, which stayed with him for the rest of his life. E. Stanley Jones, a missionary in India, would say of Gandhi: "There's only one Christian in the world today - and he's a Hindu."

We need not change our faith, or undermine that of another, simply because it differs from our own, or even because they interpret it differently than we would. What we can do - whether we are religious, spiritual, or none of the above - is show with our own lives the spirit of nonviolence in action: selfless service to one another and mutual respect.

DAY 30

I have wisdom enough to know my limitations.
– Gandhi, *Harijan,* July 23, 1938

Whereas violence asks us to regard the limitations of others and ourselves as weaknesses, knowledge of our own limitations is a strength in nonviolence, because the discipline of nonviolence, when understood as a broad "experiment with truth," gives us the capability to do something about them. We may, for example, know how to protect ourselves from having our weaknesses exploited. If you know that certain issues, words, or attitudes will push your buttons, you can prepare yourself to maintain nonviolent discipline when they come up.

Gandhi felt that Socrates was one of the greatest practitioners of nonviolence, since the philosopher was the first to admit that he was wise precisely *because* he knew "nothing." Without the pretense in our minds that we have all of the knowledge to solve all of the world's problems - not to mention our personal issues - we are free to embark on the creative path of curiosity, as real experimenters in the power of nonviolence.

DAY 31

If we could erase the "I's" and "Mine's" from religion, politics, economics, etc., we shall soon be free and bring heaven upon earth.
– Gandhi, *Young India*, September 3, 1926

What if we were to turn the current purpose of our mainstream institutions on its head? These institutions could be reformed with a mandate to serve all of life, instead of serving to aggrandize oneself or one's own allies, while never neglecting the individual's good. For example, a school would not promote individualism and competition for becoming richer than others. Rather, it would encourage students to cooperate at increasingly larger scales to build solutions to the world's toughest problems, ones which require creative and robust collaborative work, like ending war or planning healthy, livable cities. Imagine politicians lending a hand to one another, knowing that everyone's best interests would be met through service.

This shift in worldview within our institutions is not impossible - we already see examples of it every day, from B Corporations to free clinics - and it would encourage and support all of us to get along with one another in more constructive and less combative ways.

DAY 32

One cannot forgive too much.
– Gandhi, *Young India*, April 2, 1931

When Gandhi returned to South Africa for his second stay in 1897, he was not a welcomed guest. The South African port and police kept his ship quarantined for close to twenty days just off the Durban shore, as a tactic to get him and the other Indians on the boat to go back to India. When the ship was finally allowed to dock, a friend of Gandhi's came aboard and told him not to disembark until nightfall, since an angry crowd awaited him for raising so much "trouble" in the colony. Gandhi felt that secrecy was out of the question and refused to wait until darkness, stepping off the ship in full dignity, dressed proudly in Indian clothing, and accompanied by his wife and children. He was immediately surrounded by the angry mob, who began to beat him unconscious. He was saved only by the wife of the police superintendent, who happened to be passing by and stepped in with her umbrella, getting the men to go away.

The next day, Gandhi was taken to the police station, he did not press charges against those who assaulted him. He calmly stated his case: that these men were simply reacting to their government's propaganda, and it was the system he opposed, not the men who beat him. Gandhi knew that by forgiving the men, he was winning them over.

Forgiveness is a powerful tool in nonviolence. When people try to hurt us, we show them another way instead of returning the blow. If we try to do nonviolence without forgiveness, we're finished at the first insult we receive. Forgiveness requires a strong sense of self.

DAY 33

A sincere prayer can work wonders.
– Gandhi, *Young India*, March, 24, 1920

There will be times when we seem to reach the end of our capacity for love, for forgiveness, for service, for nonviolence. There will be days when we want to lose our temper and cause suffering to others. During these times, prayer can be a steady aid in unlocking our higher potential.

Praying does not mean supplicating some outside force to make our problems go away. It is more natural. In prayer, we turn inward through a practice of deep concentration, and share the problem we are facing with ourselves. And just as the body has amazing ways of healing itself naturally, the mind and spirit can work wonders together to bring up stores of energy that they reserve specifically for tough times.

In Sanskrit, God is sometimes called *kshamasagara*, a great ocean of compassion. Mystics of all stripes maintain that this is the one ocean which will never run dry; we can draw from it, over and over again. We are capable of so much more than we realize.

DAY 34

I believe that true democracy can only be an outcome of nonviolence.
– Gandhi, *Gandhi's Correspondence with the Government 1942-1944*

Violence and democracy are actually incompatible. In violence, you must force your will upon another person or group, which uproots any attempt at cultivating a democratic spirit - dignity for the human being. Contrary to the rhetoric of politicians invested in the use of violence, we can never export democracy to other countries by the force of bombs and militaries. That only replaces one form of dictatorship or terrorism with yet another.

Our challenge today is reducing violence without sacrificing democracy in the process. Fortunately, the worldwide growth of unarmed civilian peacekeeping is showing us such a way. Instead of sending in armed people who are taught to hate and fear the inhabitants of countries they are supposed to be "liberating" with "democracy," we can send in unarmed peacekeepers who function as a neutral third party to help deescalate violence, protect civilians, and support nonviolent movements. Creating security by nourishing people-powered democracy, not spreading and escalating tensions and violence, is the way of the future.

DAY 35

Violence like water, when it has an outlet, rushes forward furiously with an overwhelming force. Nonviolence cannot act madly. It is the essence of discipline.

– Gandhi, *Harijan*, March 21, 1939

A friend once told us that had he not had the nonviolent mentorship of an adult in his life at a key moment, he would have easily been persuaded to join the military. He went on to create the East Point Peace Academy, which offers trainings in the skills of nonviolence as understood by Martin Luther King, Jr., and also provides training for inmates. What does nonviolence offer as much as military training? Gandhi would unequivocally say self-discipline.

These days it seems we need self-discipline in ever greater measure, yet if the military is the only institution servicing this need, especially for young people, it is no wonder that many still find this violent institution appealing. In our current culture, the less restraint we show the more easily we're manipulated, making restraint a counter to oppression.

It takes restraint not to strike with a fist or sharp words when someone questions our dignity or otherwise harms us. Yet the corporate media and the military are literally invested in our thinking that self-restraint is the wrong road to freedom. On the contrary, we should be absolutely clear that the more self-restraint we show in nonviolence, the freer we are.

DAY 36

Those who own money now, are asked to behave like trustees holding their riches on behalf of the poor.
– Gandhi, *Modern Review*, October 1935

Gandhi was convinced it was useless to demand that people give up their wealth, as some socialists in the freedom struggle felt should happen. His answer instead was trusteeship: seeing our wealth and possessions as tools for service, not exploitation. Gandhi was the perfect example of a trustee in action: millions of rupees passed through his hands, and he never saw any of it as his, owning only a few possessions at the time of death.

Our security lies in the good of the community. When some people cannot meet even their basic needs while others have more than enough, we still have work to do. Thinking that our security comes from personal possessions and the accumulation of wealth for private pleasures actually brings us less security. Depending upon changing external circumstances can never make a person secure. Real wealth, real joy, begins with the realization that nothing on Earth really belongs to us alone.

DAY 37

Experience gained in two schools under my control has taught me that punishment does not purify; if anything, it hardens children.
– Gandhi, *Mahatma, Vol. 2*

One day, Gandhi's grandson Arun was in Johannesburg with his father, Manilal, getting their car fixed. While his father went to an appointment, Arun was to wait for the car and pick him up when it was ready. However, Arun went into a theater to watch some John Wayne films. He saw a double feature, and suddenly realized that it was way past the time to pick up his father. He decided to make up a story about the car not being ready earlier, to avoid getting in trouble. To his surprise, when he told his father what "happened," Manilal told him that he had already called the garage, and knew that the story was not true.

Disappointed that his son would lie to him, Manilal chose to walk home to the ashram, more than eighteen miles away. Arun drove behind him, at a snail's pace, for hours. The result was that Arun learned a very important lesson that no punishment could have conveyed. "That made me decide never to tell a lie," Arun said. "If he had punished me, I would have taken the punishment and decided not to get caught the next time."

DAY 38

I have no desire to cause you unnecessary embarrassment,
or any at all, so far as I can help.
– Gandhi, *Young India*, March 12, 1930

Gandhi's faith in the power of Truth was so deep that he never felt he had to embarrass his opponents to promote his cause. He believed that by consistently respecting the full human dignity of his opponent - and taking on the suffering in a situation if necessary, in an effort to bring the truth to light - his aims would be fulfilled more robustly and directly. For example, when Britain was caught up in World War II, just as the freedom struggle was gaining momentum, Gandhi either held back satyagraha or executed it symbolically, to show that they were not going away.

This principle is called non-embarrassment. If your opponent is in a position of weakness, or is distracted, it shows a lack of faith in one's powers to hit them while they're down. Wait until you have their full attention, then show them what you're made of - that is, catch them off guard with empathy and nonviolence. They probably weren't expecting it.

DAY 39

Whatever cannot be shared with the masses is taboo to me.
– Gandhi, *Harijan*, November 2, 1934

Public figures and politicians often fly around in private jets while claiming to be servants of the people. Gandhi wanted to show his dedication to the principle we today call servant leadership by living with those served, and by taking on the challenges experienced by the masses. It was a natural step for someone who caught a glimpse at the way that class privilege was used to divide people who otherwise could be working together.

Remember the 1982 film *Gandhi*? It rightly depicts his conscious turning point as a young lawyer who was kicked out of the first-class compartment of a train in South Africa, because he was of Indian origin. "But wait, I have a first-class ticket!" he protested. "Too bad," was the response. Talk about an indignant wake-up! He seethed on the train platform for hours. No one should be treated this way, or compelled to treat others this way, he thought. That was 1893, and we can say that he was thrown off of a train and into the arms of nonviolence.

Then, as Gandhi's awareness of his interconnection with others grew, he began to refuse certain privileges that the masses would not have access to. To take an example, a reporter once asked Gandhi, "Why do you travel by third-class train?" Gandhi's reply: "Because there is no fourth class yet."

DAY 40

By a long course of prayerful discipline, I have ceased for over forty years to hate anybody. I know that this is a big claim. Nevertheless, I make it in all humility.
– Gandhi, *Young India,* June 18, 1925

While Gandhi said that he ceased to hate anybody, he never denied hating the acts of people. He learned that to help them change their ways, to right the wrong of their actions, he had to dissociate people from their deeds. Everyone has worth because they are a human being.

Gandhi emphasizes that it requires discipline to move beyond hatred of people - more than just any kind of discipline, a prayerful one resting on a faith in the basic humanness in everyone. When we become aware of hatred in our minds, it is our duty to interrupt hate-filled thoughts before they become words or deeds. Better deeds would follow naturally from a mind freed from hatred; we would recondition our reactions towards separation and passivity to a more active state of seeking unity with whomever we're dealing with.

Training our minds in love is on par with liberating ourselves from the corrosive influence of hating. Nonviolence - and nonviolent resistance - is the outward form of that training.

DAY 41

Goodness becomes dynamic only when it is practiced in the face of evil.
– Gandhi, *Young India,* April 13, 1921

Let us assume that when Gandhi uses terms like "goodness" and "evil" he is referring not to people, but to conscious actions and thoughts. An action or thought is "evil" when one consciously chooses to harm another. When one consciously chooses to benefit and express care for another, that action or thought is considered "good."

The power of goodness is not tested in situations and with people who only want to benefit and help us. We put goodness to work in the face of circumstances and people who intend to do us harm. For example, it is easy to tell someone that you love and appreciate them when you are certain that they also love and appreciate you. It is much harder to do so when the other party wants to harm you. But that is just the moment when goodness can demonstrate that it is a quality of the soul, that is not dependent upon external circumstances to find its full expression.

DAY 42

It is not any single isolated act which can be called Satyagraha apart from the spirit behind.
– Gandhi, *Young India*, September 24, 1925

You cannot get far in the world of nonviolence before coming across Gene Sharp's famous list of one hundred and ninety-eight methods of nonviolent action, which includes sit-ins, reverse strikes, and pray-ins. This list evolves with each new creative act of nonviolence that takes place. But the list doesn't tell us much about what nonviolence really looks like and how it actually works. It merely gives us tactics, which while useful, cannot teach us how to maintain nonviolent discipline, let alone emphasize its value. We don't find some of the tactics, on the list, such as humiliation, nonviolent.

Nonviolence, Gandhi urges, is the spirit behind the action. To carry out nonviolence according to a list of tactics alone, protestors can actually be violent in their acts. To avoid this jeopardy, nonviolent activists must ask: Was the act intended to harm an opponent or alienate someone? Was it done out of fear instead of courage? Did it strive to maintain the dignity of all parties involved? These questions are not easy to answer. They require some minor self-knowledge, a lot of major introspection, and the humility to admit when we've made an error.

To fully see nonviolence at work, we must direct our attention to what's going on inside our hearts and minds.

DAY 43

Non-cooperation is an attempt to awaken the masses
to a sense of their dignity and power.
– Gandhi, *Young India*, February 1, 1920

When we hear requests to be "peaceful and nonviolent" from government officials during riots and times of tension, we owe it to ourselves to question their understanding of nonviolence. Do they think that nonviolence means passivity or turning to corporate media to tell us what is happening in our democracy? Calls for nonviolence from those who have, through neglect or worse, permitted violence on their side is rank hypocrisy.

Nonviolent non-cooperation means we are willing to show up in the streets when officials tell us not to do so. It means that we: refuse to believe propaganda suggesting that people have no right to express any anger, frustration, and pain caused by a violent system; put our bodies in the way of business as usual; non-cooperate with the mindset and practices that made violence possible to begin with.

We also have to ask what our movement believes nonviolence to be. Does randomly destroying property show our values, help our cause, or encourage those who would otherwise stay indoors to join us? While non-cooperation can awaken our power and dignity, we should not let it go dormant until the next problem arises. Our next, if not simultaneous steps, should always be to activate nonviolent cooperation and work towards transforming the systems that caused these problems.

DAY 44

The world today is moving towards the ideal of collective
or co-operative effort in every department of life.
– Gandhi, *Harijan*, February 5, 1942

Through her expertise of the microbial universe, evolution biologist and futurist Elisabet Sahtouris can speak about the human condition from an incredibly penetrating angle. Life, as she puts it, has been discovering and rediscovering cooperative effort for billions of years. Bacteria, for instance, tried everything they possibly could to avoid working together, iteration after iteration, experiment after experiment, until they finally turned to one another to cooperate and became capable of incredible feats. Multicellular organisms, anyone? *Finally.*

If bacteria can discover the power of nonviolence, we humans, who are infinitely more complex (and yet made of the same stuff - we are made up of ten times more bacterial cells than "human") are sure to make it there one day too. Gandhi's vision of humanity moving towards cooperation, then, is more than a whimsical wish upon the waters. As we can now point out that his claim is backed by modern science, let us take heart in the midst of this evolutionary struggle: we are well on our way forward in our great journey back home to one another.

DAY 45

What appears as truth to one person may appear as untruth to another.
– Gandhi, *Yeravda Mandir*

Have you heard the story about the blindfolded men at different places around an elephant, describing what they felt? One man standing next to a leg says, "An elephant is round and straight," while another man feeling just the tusks says, "No, an elephant is actually rather hard and curved." And so forth. There they were, each one feeling that he knew the truth yet each one experiencing something very different.

Gandhi would say that we all hold separate pieces of the truth, small "t," but by putting all our truths together, we can turn them into something much larger than any one of us can hold entirely on our own. We need to validate one another's experiences, even if our experiences widely differ.

That said, it seems to require cultivating the disciplines of nonviolence in order to be willing to acknowledge that others have an experience that deserves validation. Once we get there, we need to be just as willing to hold our own truth as equally valid. Our truths never negate one another, but in some way or another reinforce each other. It is not you against me or me against you; it is you and me against the problem (in other words: it's you and me working together to resolve the problem).

DAY 46

Exploitation is the essence of violence.
– Gandhi, *Harijan,* August 25, 1939

At the root of exploitation is the worldview of separateness, the idea that we can gain some kind of personal benefit by harming others. In nonviolence, we want to turn exploitation on its head with the realization that no one truly benefits from hurting others. Those who wish to bring nonviolence into the world must recognize our collusion with exploitative systems and practices, to avoid them wherever possible - from our food production to high rents and the costs of our basic needs; from our clothing choices to the dynamics of our personal relationships.

Even in our struggles for justice, we cannot set up a new system based on the worldview of separateness. To combat exploitation, we must make an ongoing effort to establish the real welfare of the whole, which includes our own wellbeing. Here is a thought for us to keep in mind: If the essence of violence is exploitation, the essence of nonviolence is service.

DAY 47

The spirit of democracy cannot be established in the midst of terrorism, whether governmental or popular.
– Gandhi, *Young India*, February 23, 1921

Martin Luther King, Jr.'s *Stride Toward Freedom: The Montgomery Story* recounts an amazing event toward the end of the African American freedom struggle of the 1960s. The Ku Klux Klan tried to regain its power over a community of color by driving through it one night. Instead of cowering indoors (up to then the usual response to a "Klan ride"), people stood on their porches and waved, asked their hooded guests if they needed directions. People were not afraid this time, and the unexpected happened: the Klansmen turned their cars around and left.

The objective of terrorism is to make people so fearful that they comply with whatever is demanded of them, giving up their power and their choices. Violence, Gandhi would say, is no way to respond to this situation, because it, too, tries to cow others into submission. Tragically and unfortunately, many liberation struggles end by restructuring the initial violence.

The way to uphold the spirit of democracy, Gandhi insisted, was by refusing to submit to the mechanisms of terror, whatever its source. Toward this end, he helped Indians look on jail time as a badge of honor. Ultimately, he maintained that dying - not killing - in the cause of nonviolence was the highest bravery. Nonviolence is not only the way to dislodge a domineering regime, he pointed out; it's a way to dislodge the terror on which it's based.

DAY 48

If we want to cultivate a true spirit of democracy,
we cannot afford to be intolerant.
– Gandhi, *Young India,* February 2, 1921

The spirit of democracy is based on valuing the individual. To be intolerant of anyone based on our particular likes, dislikes, or even fears, is therefore a negation of that spirit. At the same time, we cannot tolerate acts of injustice and harm in our midst. But even in our intolerance of violence, we must be wary of recreating the very system and mindset it seeks to dismantle. The reminder that we are against the evil and not the person is our best way to do so.

It must also be said that in the way of human relationships, the opposite of intolerance is not tolerance. Mere tolerance can connote a sense of superiority of one group "allowing for" the existence of another. *I don't like or support what you do, but I have to tolerate it.* The real opposite of intolerance is mutual understanding, the realization of our interconnectedness on deeper and deeper levels. This is why Gandhi wanted children to do a reverential study of other religions and not just learn about the facts of them. Think of how much bloodshed that would have saved!

DAY 49

A Swadeshi will learn to do without hundreds of things which today he considers necessary.
– Gandhi, *Selected Writings of Mahatma Gandhi*

Many people still believe that localism, or *swadeshi*, is a far-fetched notion. Certainly, it is not without its complexities, but it is not beyond us to strive towards it regularly, even if we do not, or cannot, attain its full realization.

Gandhi is suggesting that when we commit ourselves to localism, we will no doubt have to put up with some inconveniences (convenience being, after all, a key promise of consumerism). Think of all the things we have come to depend on that are made thousands of miles from where we live.

If we are truly committed to ending exploitation, of people and the planet, we will indeed need to put up with those personal inconveniences, at least temporarily, while holding onto the vision that if we lack something locally, we may be able to produce it locally, and if not, Gandhi himself was not opposed to a degree of interdependency, or what we'd call "fair trade." Still, ending exploitation requires our willingness to forgo many things we think are necessary (do we *really* need a new cell phone or a second car?). Perhaps the greatest experiment in nonviolence upon which all of us can embark is the voluntary reduction of our desires and wants. In the context of a spiritual practice, this can be liberating.

DAY 50

The golden way is to be friends with the world and to regard the whole human family like members of one family.
– Gandhi, *Young India,* May 11, 1921

The family is often a challenging place to practice nonviolence, especially if there are standing conflicts yet to be resolved. Brother and sister no longer talk; mother and daughter are alienated; son never forgave father for his problems; etc. A tendency when there is such conflict is to move away from people, avoiding them whenever possible and at best wishing them well. Family relationships, however, matter in nonviolent psychology, and even strategy, because they provide a firm grounding for expanding our ability to engage nonviolence with those outside our immediate sphere

While Gandhi tells us to expand our vision to include the whole world as members of our own family, he is not telling us to love only anonymous people to whom we may never speak; who may never insult us, or forget something important to us, or ask us to do something we'd prefer not doing. He is telling us to build a firm foundation for nonviolence, respect, and dignity in our own families - with people who will rub against our self-will from time to time, and from there, we cannot help but widen our awareness to bring others into that circle. What does it mean to treat one's family as the whole world, and the whole world as one's own family? It's a subtle but worthy challenge for all of us to consider.

DAY 51

Mere abstention from physical violence will not meet our purpose.
– Gandhi, *Harijan,* June 10, 1939

Perhaps as a child you learned this retort to insults: "Sticks and stones will break my bones, but words will never harm me." Experience, however, is a different matter - words do hurt. Even loving words, when said in a tone that confers less dignity to us than we are worth, can do harm

Similarly, thoughts can also hurt us. If someone in our life does not believe us to be worthy of their time and love, it can cause alienation and psychological harm. We must acknowledge that emotional violence is as harmful as physical violence, if not more so, since we cannot see its effects immediately

Since a human being is an integral whole of mind, body, and spirit, our nonviolence must also be integral. Abstaining from physical violence is only one stage of development. We have to abstain from spiritual and emotional violence too. By striving to cultivate our nonviolence into deeper, unseen parts of ourselves, we can feel its power and effectiveness increase as well. And there will come a time in all of our lives and movements when we need to draw on those deeper resources.

DAY 52

Service is not possible unless it is rooted in love, or ahimsa.
– Gandhi, *Truth is God*

Everywhere we go, we hear the word "service." Our banks provide various services; our clothing and grocery stores are there to serve us. Even the military is called "service." Banks, etc. are not in business to serve their clients so much as to make a profit. And the military? This is "service" of one's own group very much at the expense of others, and it exploits a noble concept for personal gain

In this system, we are told that the more money you have, the more service you get. But we are also lulled into letting others make our choices for us. *Don't worry about the wars we wage. Actually, don't even think about them; we'll think about them for you.* Let's not buy into it - literally!

Gandhi raises the bar when he maintains that service must be rooted in love, or ahimsa. Can we have servicemen and women who do not learn hatred but cultural sensitivity and nonviolence? Can we have relationships in which those who have more see themselves at the service of those who have less? Of course we can, and we have many examples of people doing just that. The key, Gandhi would say, is changing how we view service, so it becomes a force to uplift all concerned.

DAY 53

The law of love will work, just as the law of gravitation will work, whether we accept it or not.
– Gandhi, *The Nation's Voice, Part II*

Gandhi was a scientist in regards to the practice of nonviolence. He carried out precise experiments in every aspect of his life, driven by a deep desire to realize its promise: liberation. Many people told him that nonviolence was unrealistic and wouldn't work (sound familiar?). To these skeptics, Gandhi would humbly state: "the law of love will work" whether we are aware of it or not, whether we accept it or not

The spirit was firmly Gandhi's domain: If there are laws of the universe that apply to the body, such as gravity, there are also laws that govern the spirit. His claim that "love works" was not hypothetical, hopeful, or merely sentimental; it was the fruit of direct experience and systematic practice in working out this law on the widest scale possible.

DAY 54

I advise women to resort to civil rebellion against
all undesirable and unworthy restraints.
– Gandhi, *Harijan*, March 23, 1947

The celebration of Holi announces the arrival of springtime. Rose petals, marigolds, and multihued powders are tossed in the air, signifying renewal, forgiveness, and the joy of being alive. Widows, however, are frowned upon for participating in Holi, due to ancient superstitions suggesting that their presence in religious celebrations is polluting - an unworthy restraint upon them, to be sure. Many widows are outright rejected by their families and left to fend for themselves

Gandhi, who worked hard on the question of the treatment of widows, would be pleased to hear that widows are rebelling against dehumanizing treatment. In Vrindavan, India, "the town of widows," groups of widows who have retired into the town's ashrams have participated in the Holi festival. The white saris that widows must usually wear turned vibrant from the colorful powders tossed at them. The widows danced, and even wore make-up, to mark the special occasion

As the principle goes in nonviolence: "Ask what they are holding over you. Renounce that, and you are free." These widows are showing us that by renouncing the taboo that looms over their existence, they, if even for just a day, experience a freedom that shows them the way forward - in joy, playfulness, and power.

DAY 55

Repression itself affords a training in Satyagraha, even as an unsought war affords a training for the soldier.
– Gandhi, *Harijan*, April 8, 1939

A common misconception is that nonviolence will be met with gentle words and actions from those to whom it is offered. This is rarely, if ever, the case, especially when it comes to challenging systems built on the foundations of violence, such as police or military, on which so many rely for their sense of security. If we are not prepared for violent repression from the outset, we will be in for some unhappy surprises, and we might mistakenly decide that nonviolence is ineffective because it cannot protect us from being harmed

Nonviolence is not a tool to keep us from being harmed. It is a tool to teach us how to stop the harm of others and ourselves, by putting ourselves in its way. James Lawson, during the African American freedom struggle of the 1960s for example, trained civil rights activists through role-plays, to prepare them to maintain nonviolent discipline amidst violent reactions

There is no need to court martyrdom. In the planning stage of mass nonviolent resistance, we need to make sure there are monitors on hand to deal with outbursts of undue violence; people present from the movement who are prepared to offer medical and psychological/spiritual support; journalists on hand to tell the story of nonviolence as it happens; and those who can offer the ever-practical ride home from jail.

DAY 56

I am a humble explorer of the science of nonviolence.
– Gandhi, *Young India*, November 20, 1924

Nonviolence: a strategy for some people, a moral imperative for others. For Gandhi, it was mainly a science. Understanding that the fundamental basis of science is the spirit of hypothesis and experimentation, he took upon himself great challenges with the detachment needed to realize what went wrong, what to adjust, and how to replicate the experiment as needed. Like a good scientist, he was aware that "the instrument of observation" affected the results of the experiment. For example, you get different results from a microscope than you will a telescope. And smudges on the lenses of either of these instruments would lead to problematic findings. Similarly, if the person behind the microscope does not know what they are seeing, they could overlook important findings

So it is in nonviolence: we are the instruments of experimentation and observation. The more resentment in our hearts, the more we affect the results of our action. The more relaxed we are in a given situation - even if we are resisting and being firm with someone - the better we will influence the result. Gandhi was talking about the science of nonviolence before science could back up his unique form of social research. However, over the past thirty years, science has been giving us a much more inspiring picture of how nonviolence

actually works, from quantum physics to mirror neurons.

DAY 57

A man who aspires after that cannot keep out of any field of life.
– Gandhi, *Autobiography: The Story of My Experiments with Truth*

Gandhi did not like being labeled. Any label, however convenient for some purposes, would be an artificial limitation. "Are you a spiritual teacher or a politician?" people would ask him, implying that if he was one, then he had no business being the other. Yet for someone striving for union, such attempted dualities were of little interest at best and misleading at worst. At the same time, Gandhi felt that the honorific title Mahatma was a burden to him. He would easily agree with Dorothy Day's famous quip: "Don't call me a Saint. I don't want to be dismissed that easily."

The "Mahatma" maintains that his pursuit of Truth led him into the various areas of life (politics, religion, education, health), and that he could not do otherwise because of the nature of Truth itself. Certainly feminists and other social justice activists today will say the same thing: we cannot separate the political from the personal. Whatever we do in our personal lives is accountable to the system at large.

DAY 58

My seventy years' experience has taught me that the truly great are often those of whom and of whose greatness the world knows nothing during their lifetime.
– Gandhi, *Harijan,* December 10, 1938

You may know about the grave of the Unknown Soldier, but have you come across a national monument to the Unknown Peacemaker? We should have a monument for the latter in every town and city across our country, because all of us have been moved and inspired by such a person. Maybe this peacemaker was a grandmother, whose gentle words taught you self-confidence. Or a teacher who encouraged you to think more deeply or tenderly. Maybe the peacemaker was a colleague who *really* listened to you. Or that total stranger who kept you out of harm's way

This peacemaker is inside all of us, and each day our deeds and actions ripple out into the lives of those we encounter. This interconnection, this unconscious form of service, is a gift we all receive, just for having lived. While invisible, this peacemaking work is unstoppable in its healing powers.

DAY 59

Men generally hesitate to make a beginning if they feel that the objective cannot be had in its entirety. Such an attitude of mind is in reality a bar to progress.
– Gandhi, *Harijan,* November 11, 1940

There are many misconceptions about nonviolence, but one of the most disempowering myths goes something like: "To practice nonviolence, you must be perfect, or at least near to it." We have heard people say that they were "too angry" to be nonviolent, or who have suggested that those who strive for the nonviolent ideal are hypocritical if they get angry. But if nonviolence were for the "perfect," then where is the hope for any of us?

The reality is, nonviolence is the practice of converting one's anger to creative uses. We're inspired when we hear that anyone has taken up the path, because what they are in for is going to be as psychologically and spiritually freeing as it is, at times, tiring and heartbreaking. It is not easy to forgive a person when everything inside of you is goading to you resent, distrust, or move away from them. But in nonviolence we do just that - we forgive, because we are not willing to live by the conditioning of separation so many of us have come to accept as normal.

We do not become wholly nonviolent without conflict. A state without conflict simply does not exist. So should you throw in the towel and say that nonviolence is not for you? Or do you see conflict as an opportunity to work your heart muscles and grow more loving and supportive?

DAY 60

Has not the atom bomb proved the futility of all violence?
– Gandhi, *Harijan*, March 10, 1946

The twentieth century witnessed moments in which nonviolence soared to giddying heights and violence brought us down to unfathomed lows. It is an amazing contrast.

When Gandhi heard that the United States had used the atomic bomb in Japan, he said that he sat still and silent. "I did not move a muscle when I first heard that the atom bomb had wiped out Hiroshima," he said. "On the contrary, I said to myself, 'Unless now the world adopts nonviolence, it will spell certain suicide for mankind.'"

When asked if the destruction of Hiroshima had exploded his faith in nonviolence, Gandhi said that such a faith was the only thing that the atom bomb could not destroy. He advocated for states to disarm, noting that the courage it required in a climate of violence would be enormous, but that the nation that could do it would catalyze a transformational shift. He was presupposing a deeper understanding of who we are, a faith in ourselves that makes that level of courage real as well as available to us.

It is not a coincidence that the bombs were given human names ("Little Boy" and "Fat Man"), while the people of Japan were not seen as people at all. We must carry the people of Japan in our hearts, never forgetting what occurred and never letting it happen again. Nonviolence is the only way.

DAY 61

Independence must begin at the bottom.
– Gandhi, *Harijan,* July 28, 1946

On April 6, 1930, the Great Salt March reached the shore in Dandi, eighty thousand people strong. The marchers' aim was to break the colonial law prohibiting Indians from making salt without permission from the British. Gandhi picked up a lump of salt and addressed the crowd:

> Now that the technical or ceremonial breach of the salt law has been committed, it is open to anyone who would take the risk of prosecution under the salt law to manufacture salt, wherever he wishes and wherever it is convenient. My advice is that the workers should everywhere make use of it and instruct the villagers likewise, telling the villager at the same time that he runs the risk of being prosecuted. In other words, the villager should be fully instructed as to the incidence of the salt tax, and the manner of breaking the laws and regulations connected with it, so as to have the salt tax repealed.

Violent "democracy building" tries to impose independence from the top-down. Gandhi helps us see that such dependency makes us less free. The power of nonviolence lies in its being a bottom-up model of independence: We're already free, and we are willing to show you this is true. Freedom is the essence of being human. The salt law was not in fact repealed as a result of the campaign, though the marchers showed the Indian people that they were not subject to British laws.

DAY 62

All activity for stopping war must prove fruitless so long as the causes of war are not understood and radically dealt with.
– Gandhi, *Harijan,* February 11, 1939

A friend of ours once had a New Yorker cartoon tacked to his office door. It depicted several individuals throwing a plastic bottle into a trash can that was overflowing with them, each person saying, "It's only one bottle; it doesn't make a difference." But as we know, it *does* make a difference, as the "trash islands" of plastic in the Pacific Ocean illustrate.

What we do individually matters, because we participate in a collective. We can also use this notion in nonviolence, in relation to how we channel our emotions into destructive or constructive institutions. Addressing the fear, greed, and anger within ourselves might not seem like a priority with so much in the world needing our attention. Yet Gandhi tells us that to end war and exploitation, we must get to its roots: our own minds.

What is mass incarceration if not the institutionalization of mass fear? What is corporate exploitation if not the institutionalization of mass greed? What is war if not the institutionalization of mass anger? At the same time, what is love if not the ultimate transformation of our destructive drives into a growing force for generosity, kindness, and courage?

DAY 63

The extension of the law of nonviolence in the domain of economics means nothing less than the introduction of moral values as a factor to be considered in regulating international commerce.
– Gandhi, *Young India*, December 26, 1924

Morality in economics sounds like an oxymoron. But consider the boycott: it is a tool to regulate economics along the lines of moral values (we will not buy your product if you exploit labor, or use poisons or GMOs to produce it). Getting morality into economics is a challenge, but let us all be intrigued by imagining what economics would look like if moral values were not an afterthought or a reason for protest, but a guideline and point of departure. Where better to begin than with the abiding happiness that comes from helping others?

The Kingdom of Bhutan introduced the Gross National Happiness Index to the world in 1972 as an alternative to the Gross National Product. Launched as an effort to integrate primarily Buddhist spiritual values into their national vision, the Happiness Index spearheaded a movement, with results such as the United Nations including happiness as a key value in its global development agenda in 2011.

Gandhi was onto this idea early. With ads constantly trying to sell us an *idea* of happiness through endless consumption, and even violence, wouldn't nonviolence be an actual indicator of our happiness? It's time we measured wealth where it really resides.

DAY 64

If I could persuade myself that I could find [God] in a Himalayan cave, I would proceed there immediately. But I know I cannot find [God] apart from humanity.
– Gandhi, *Harijan,* August 29, 1936

Gandhi was known as a karma yogi, because his spiritual path was one of engagement and selfless action. Does this mean that everyone must be on this same path? For the vast majority of us living in families, and who have commitments and jobs, we do not need to renounce these relationships and responsibilities to attain spiritual wisdom.

When we resort to isolation, we have to ask whether we are hiding from difficult situations and obligations out of a sense of giving up on others and ourselves. We may "escape" to the most isolated corners of the world, but if we go with resentment or fear in our hearts, we will be taking our problems with us - and they will still be with us when we return. If we want to grow spiritually, we must learn to live together. We can find the resources we need to do that within our own, and one another's, hearts.

DAY 65

I believe in the conversion of mankind, not its destruction.
– Gandhi, *The Collected Works for Mahatma Gandhi, Vol. XXV*

The prison system is one of the most stark institutional examples of the urgent need to change our vision of who we are as human beings. This retributive justice model destroys dignity and self-respect, and it ironically pretends to offer security. Yet it is our human dignity and self-respect that make us secure. By undercutting these two fundamental qualities of the spirit, we undermine the possibility of a nonviolent future. But this does not need to be the case.

We can draw from Gandhi's wisdom, holding fast to the notion that with enough time, and enough compassion, we can convert and transform our negative impulses into powerfully constructive channels. By allowing this process to take its course, as we see in restorative justice practices, we evolve away from the illusion that violence is necessary in our dealings with others - and ourselves. That is something we can turn into an institution on a massive scale. With it, we affirm the dignity of every human life and make ourselves more secure, more fulfilled, and even smarter in the process.

DAY 66

Trusting one another, however, can never mean trusting with the lips and mistrusting with the heart.
– Gandhi, *The Collected Works for Mahatma Gandhi, Vol. XXV*

How can we build a system of cooperation and empathy while at the same time distrusting those with whom we collaborate? Trust is fundamental to nonviolent action. As the Buddha said, "trust is the best of relationships."

But when it comes to leadership in nonviolent movements, might we be trusting one another with our lips while mistrusting one another with our hearts? The "everyone's a leader" approach we see in the United States in particular seems to be empowerment on the surface, but we wonder if it actually hides our distrust of one another.

Choosing and working with a leader, or leadership group, after all, is the only way we can follow through on an agreed-upon strategic agenda. Instead of eschewing leadership in the name of empowerment, we might reassess how we choose leaders for nonviolent movements, what leadership qualities we seek in that person/people, and why we trust them once we select them. This does not mean *not* holding them accountable, though it really does mean trusting. What could be more empowering than trusting one another in our movements?

DAY 67

The force of love is the same as the force of the soul or truth. We have evidence of it working at every step. The universe would disappear without the existence of that force.

– Gandhi, *Hind Swaraj*

What passes for love in popular entertainment often has very little to do with what Gandhi means by the force of love. What we frequently see is an intersection of coercion, aggression, mere physical desire, passivity ("falling in love" as though it took no work, or putting up with abuse in the name of "loving" someone), selfishness, and manipulation pretending to be love.

More like a skill and an art, love is active, sincere, and simple. When consciously harnessed and applied to each of our relationships, it becomes identical with the practice of nonviolence. Capable as we all are of this kind of love, we nonetheless have to develop it daily to know its full potential.

DAY 68

My life is an indivisible whole, and all my activities
run into one another; and they all have their rise
in my insatiable love of mankind.
– Gandhi, *The Message of Mahatma Gandhi*

A participant in a workshop we once hosted asked whether there could be conflict without anger. The short answer is a big "probably not." Anger itself is a neutral force. It can be hideously destructive, but we can also turn it into fuel for creative, positive uses. At its best, anger is a savvy messenger, telling us that a situation is rich with transformative potential for ourselves and others, as long as we harness it in a constructive direction.

The lesson on conserving anger is probably the most important gift of Gandhi's legacy: who among us doesn't have negative, disruptive drives in their consciousness? Transforming anger into a creative force is not only an explanation for the uncanny power of nonviolence, but an incredible source of hope for ourselves and our world.

DAY 69

Non-cooperation is the quickest method of creating public opinion.
– Gandhi, *Mind of Mahatma Gandhi*

Non-cooperation does not always mean stopping traffic or getting arrested. In fact, such tactics can alienate people who may be sympathetic. And what about who is able and willing to get arrested? Usually not those who are undocumented or who would prefer to stay out of jail because they have been incarcerated in the past, even if the protests are being done for their wellbeing. While such actions are certainly the fruit of noble intentions, and have seen brilliant successes here and there, they tend to be more disruptive in the end than constructive.

Non-cooperation has another face, though. Whenever we go against a prevailing social impulse like greed or retribution, we are non-cooperating with the worldview that we are separate from one another. So we are, in short, non-cooperating with violence. This does not look like a mass protest; it looks like one person helping another or a mother holding back a harsh word and giving an encouraging one instead. It looks like someone sharing their resources with someone who has less.

Our culture tells us that we are greedy and need to compete and fight with others for resources that are in short supply. When we share what we have, work together, and expect ourselves to be empathic instead of selfish, non-cooperation suddenly becomes available to everyone, and it transforms the public's opinion of itself.

DAY 70

No propaganda can be allowed which reviles other religions.
– Gandhi, *Young India,* May 29, 1924

The dehumanization of groups of people based on religions into which we were born is a step in the direction of genocide. We've seen this cruelty in action, not just in World War II, but also in post-9/11 America.

While we, this book's authors, are not Muslim ourselves, it deeply hurts us to see Muslim communities targeted - and the religion itself on trial, a form of terror to Muslims. This treatment is dishonest and violent, and we - whatever our religious background, Muslim or not - do not have to go along with it. We can reach out to one another; we can speak up when we witness something inappropriate; and we can let it sink in that security is found and realized when we help make others secure.

DAY 71

I believe in the essential unity of humanity, and
for that matter, all that lives.
– Gandhi, *Young India*, September 3, 1925

For nonviolent institutions to be possible, they must be built on a cultural foundation of respect and reverence for the human experience.

Does being human mean we are mere consumers? Do we see ourselves as simple automatons who, in the words of Neil Postman, are "entertaining ourselves to death" in front of our screens? Is humanity destined to war at all levels? Or, can we find and agree on a far more inspiring, far more realistic conception of the human experience?

The Nguni Bantu linguistic family in southern Africa offers a word to draw from: *ubuntu* (sounds like "oo-boon-too"). Its literal translation is most closely related to terms such as "human-ness" and "human-kindness," though as ubuntu has become popularized, it has come to mean that we express our humanness only through other human beings: "I am because you are."

Our wellbeing is caught up in the web of life around us. Conversely, when we dehumanize others, we dehumanize ourselves. We can learn how to acknowledge this interconnection faster, at ever-deepening levels, and harness it to guide us into "right action," to use a Buddhist term. Wouldn't that recognition, whether on an individual or massive scale, be one of our greatest victories?

DAY 72

Make your hearts as broad as the ocean.
– Gandhi, *Young India,* January 1, 1925

Compassion is as essential to nonviolence as dehumanization is to violence. The word "compassion" derives from Latin, and it means "to suffer with." To paraphrase religious scholar Karen Armstrong, to act with compassion is "to put yourself in the shoes of another, and take the journey with them." Compassion is one of those infinite resources we possess, even if it does not always feel that way. Like love, it a difficult but valuable skill. The more of it we give, the more of it we have at our disposal.

The primary ingredient in cultivating compassion is breaking down any faulty assumptions about it. Some people say their capacity for compassion is finite and is therefore reserved for those who "deserve" it. Others believe that to be compassionate is to be naive or weak. Such misconceptions arise when we fail to see compassion as a quality of strength and power that we need to develop and use.

Gandhi is asking us to open our hearts wide so we can include everyone in our sense of compassion - victims and perpetrators, those who exploit and the exploited. When we do, we will find new insights into making our nonviolent efforts more effective, whether that is through our daily actions or mass movements.

DAY 73

Since Satyagraha is one of the most powerful methods of direct action, a Satyagrahi exhausts all other means before he resorts to Satyagraha.
– Gandhi, *Young India,* October 20, 1927

If we choose a form of pressure incommensurate with a situation - fasting right off the bat, for instance, before we've even tried to dialogue - we can do more harm than good, actually weakening ourselves when we need our energies to grow.

There are many possibilities for nonviolent action, and not every tool we have will be right for a given stage. A key example is when some twelve million people worldwide came out into the streets to protest the United States' invasion of Iraq in 2003, but then-President George W. Bush dismissed them (us) as a mere "focus group." It was a clear signal that the time for protest was over and the time for satyagraha had arrived. We did not understand that, nor were we prepared to escalate, and what resulted was as escalation of violence at home and across the world.

When we can get beneath our initial adrenal response to injustice, we can access our reason and make strategic choices that utilize our personal energies for maximum effect. As Martin Luther King, Jr. famously noted, their movement did not lead to outbursts or repressions of anger: "Yet nonviolent resistance caused no explosions of anger...it controlled anger and released it under discipline for maximum effect." Add timing into the mix, and you've got an unstoppable movement.

DAY 74

Before they dare to think of swaraj they must be brave enough to love one another.
– Gandhi, *Young India*, September 29, 1924

What does love of a nation or a larger social order look like when there is no love among those living in it? Gandhi was so concerned with this dilemma that in 1924, he told readers of his *Young India* newspaper to redirect their focus inward. A change of heart, he said, is desired from the British, certainly, and he noted that while such a change had yet to come, there should in the meantime be a definite change of heart between Hindus and Muslims.

Gandhi suggested that violence between them could be overcome if they could only overcome their own fears and insecurities. In a similar vein, he spoke about the need "to tolerate one another's religion, even prejudices and superstitions, and to trust one another," something that "requires faith in oneself."

Today, Gandhi's lessons can be applied to any two (or more) parties in conflict who have a similar, larger goal. Take climate change, for example. It affects everyone, but how can we confront it collectively and effectively without confronting our sense of alienation from one another?

A change of heart is not a one-time event. We should be brave enough to see it as a daily practice, an ever-renewed commitment.

DAY 75

Everyone should realize the secret that oppression thrives only when the oppressed submit to it.
– Gandhi, *Mahatma, Vol. 7*

This is where Gandhi's vision overlaps with that of the "strategic" school of nonviolence that emphasizes the withdrawal of consent as the major power of nonviolence. This idea goes back to the French philosopher Étienne de La Boétie and his sixteenth-century book *Discourse on Voluntary Servitude.*

When we master our fear of the dictator, and rub our eyes and realize that we have given our consent to his rule, he has lost his hold over us. Add the magic formula of remembering the humanity of your opponent while refusing his injustice, and you have Gandhian nonviolence in a nutshell.

DAY 76

I can say with confidence that if the world is to have peace, nonviolence is the means to that end and no other.
– Gandhi, *Harijan*, July 20, 1947

Aristophanes, the Greek comic playwright, used his craft as a means to open the hearts and minds of his audience to urgent truths, and his ancient work remains relevant to this day. In his play *Peace*, written to sound a note of caution at the signing of the Peace of Nicias that ended the ten-year Peloponnesian War, the characters are tasked with rescuing the goddess Peace, who has been taken captive and hidden in a cave by the god War.

At a moment of War's inattention (he has gone to find a new pestle for his mortar to "crush the Greeks to a paste"), the people realize that they have an opportunity to rescue Peace. They are so happy and excited about the opportunity that they begin dancing and running about before they've finished the job. Peace has not even been rescued, yet they are celebrating. Indeed, they end up being more hindrance than help. Peace is eventually rescued, thanks to the hard-working farmers who intervene, and Hermes helps Peace explain why she went away: she had been ignored and silenced by politicians for years on end (does any of this sound familiar?).

The moral of the story is that if we are to rescue Peace today, let us not get in the way of her full return by stopping short of what needs to take place, which as Gandhi points out, is a complete turn towards nonviolence in every sector of our lives.

DAY 77

Victory is impossible until we are able to keep our temper under the gravest provocation.
– Gandhi, *Young India*, August, 25, 1921

In the summer of 2014, we visited At-Tuwani, a village in the occupied West Bank of Palestine. From within this impoverished village of sheep herders has sprung some of the most hopeful stories of resistance to the cruelty of the settlements around their community (children must be accompanied to school to be saved from physical attack, including bullets, from extremists from the neighboring as well as illegal settlement). We were graciously welcomed in the home of Hafez Jawal, who is often called the "Gandhi of Palestine." He told us that for those living in At-Tuwani, the formula is simple: "existence is resistance."

Hafez took us on a short tour of this ancient town early one morning. The soil was rocky and sheep were roaming. He pointed to a village across the hill that did not have electricity. The villagers of At-Tuwani built their neighbors a tower to receive electricity, and it was destroyed by the Israeli military overnight. It was clear to us that the military was trying to provoke the villagers into violence. Hafez looked at us with a fire and determination in his eyes and said, "They will never provoke me into violence." Victory belongs to Hafez.

DAY 78

True friendship is an identity of souls rarely to be found in this world.
– Gandhi, *The Story of My Experiments With Truth An Autobiography*

"Friendship" is a word that is often recklessly tossed around. In Gandhi's vision, however, there can be no friendship without nonviolence. There can be bonding; we bond with one another sometimes in violent practices. Think of the bonding of soldiers in combat, which can be intense, but remains limited because it depends on bonding against an "other."

True friendship is a skill. It is also a kind of vow. When we promise our friendship to another person, we are telling them that our love for them will be unconditional; that we want to be better people through the bond, and we need a mirror for ourselves - someone who will help us remember why we are here, and who will stand up to us when we have made a mistake.

This type of friendship need not stop with two people - it can be a model for the "beloved community." Nonviolence provides the exact tools needed to build community in this way, where healing, empowerment, and honest communication take precedence over separateness.

DAY 79

We cannot command results; we can only strive.
– Gandhi, *Young India*, January 8, 1925

Striving in nonviolence is hard work, and we all need encouragement. But homework? You got it. Gandhi gave his grandson Arun homework to help him gain the inner strength he needed to keep on striving. He counseled Arun to keep a large sheet of paper in his room, and each evening to sketch out a sort of genealogical "family tree" of the day's violence. He told him to write on one side of the paper "Physical" and on the other side "Passive" and to keep track of what he witnessed, heard, did, and felt.

Gandhi wanted Arun to observe from an early age how much we all participate in forms of violence without being aware of it. Violence, Gandhi believed, can happen in our own hearts as well as in the world around us. Arun noted that this daily exercise did indeed help him see his own acts of violence more clearly, and it ingrained in him an awareness of the often unacknowledged relationship between passive and physical forms of violence (passive violence, he realized, often leads to physical violence). With such powerful and personal consciousness-raising information, he said that he could then take actions to transform himself, little by little, day by day.

DAY 80

We do not exaggerate when we say that life is a mere bubble.
– Gandhi, *Young India*, October 16, 1935

It is a paradox that human life is as fragile as it is powerful. Our capacity for love, forgiveness, compassion, and nonviolence knows no limits. From where does such power come?

Gandhi compared our existence to the image of a vast ocean, where the human being is a "mere bubble," seemingly insignificant yet ever powerful, participating in something much greater than itself. The human being does not create the world; rather, existence expresses itself through us.

Gandhi would direct us to share in the dignity of humanity. Serve and live for others, he would likely tell us today, and never lose sight of respect for yourself. For the more we alienate ourselves from one another, the more we dry up, like drops taken from the ocean.

DAY 81

Avoidance of all relationship with the opposing power can never be a Satyagrahi's object, but the transformation or purification of that relationship.

– Gandhi, *Harijan*, April 29, 1939

Nonviolence is a question of relationships, so try to never alienate your so-called opponent. Recalling the Egyptian Tahrir Square revolution, where the military and police stepped down from their roles defending the regime to join the people, well-known Syrian cartoon artist Hani Abbas created images depicting the regime's soldiers as ordinary people who love simple things, such as the scent of a beautiful flower on the ground in front of their ranks. The message? You want freedom as much as we do. Join us.

This kind of nonviolent conversion takes time. It won't happen, say, in a flash at the front lines of a direct action, when police are confronted with sensory overload as protesters start marching forward at them. It happens when nonviolence is allowed to run its full course: when protestors come forward, day in and day out, as we saw in the case of the Dharsana Salt Works in Gandhi's day. It happens when the defenders of a violent regime are not depicted as the "bad guys" to hate, but as good guys who have been convinced - or trained (see Lt. Col. Dave Grossman's book *On Killing: The Psychological Cost of Learning to Kill in War and Society*) - to do things that they themselves know, on some level, are bad.

The satyagrahi's duty is to show a higher form of courage, bravery, discipline, and devotion - but it must be within the framework of a larger, strategic vision that truly aims for the wellbeing of everyone.

DAY 82

The truth is that cowardice itself is violence of a subtle type and therefore dangerous and far more difficult to eradicate than the habit of physical violence.
– Gandhi, *The Collected Works of Mahatma Gandhi*

That cowardice is a form of violence can be counterintuitive. Wouldn't it be nonviolent, for example, to avoid a fight? As Gandhi had it, no: In avoiding our conflicts, we affirm the power of violence over us (or more simply, its power). The nonviolent way is to defy violence, to master our fear of it as far as possible.

What's true on this level of principle is also what's effective on the level of strategy: people who cringe under tyranny only perpetuate it. When we master our fear and defy violence - without causing injury to those carrying it out - we dissipate its power through our own, and very different, power.

DAY 83

How can there be room for distinctions of high and low where there is this all embracing fundamental unity underlying the outward diversity?
– Gandhi, *Young India,* September 24, 1921

The word "unity" can make some people cringe. It can also lead to overlooking the experiences of those who have been systematically oppressed, ignored, and forgotten. In this sense, the word is usually just a cover for uniformity, the unfortunate notion that we have to be the same to not be in conflict. That so-called unity is perpetuated by the violent worldview.

For democracy to be possible, Gandhi maintained, it must be built on a foundation of unity-in-diversity. This revolutionary concept considers a human being as body, mind, and spirit. On the physical plane, diversity is not only natural, it's desirable - it's the expression of the infinite complexity and creativity of the universe. On the level of mind, we strive for mutual understanding, which can only come from the recognition that on the level of spirit, we are neither fragmented nor existentially and forever separated from one another. On the spirit level we are one, and in order to realize it, paradoxical as it may sound, diversity must be embraced and honored on the surface, from physical appearance and wealth to our opinions.

DAY 84

I shall lose my usefulness the moment I stifle
the still small voice within.
– Gandhi, *Young India*, September 24, 1921

Mindfulness is popping up in schools, boardrooms, and even the military. Many people feel positive about this new culture intended to help us "succeed," while others take pause at what they call the "McMindfulness" movement, pointing to the problematic issues it might take for granted.

For example, who is defining success? Are we using "mindfulness" to teach people to love money? If so, we are using "mindfulness" as a means towards greed. Are we bringing mindfulness into low-income schools to help students to "not be violent," without any curiosity about why students may not be comfortable within our current educational system? If so, we are using "mindfulness" as a means for passivity and classist exploitation.

Mindfulness - the real deal - is about achieving a sense of conscience. Until what is currently called mindfulness becomes the practice of listening to our "still small voice," it is little more than a gimmick to make us feel more comfortable with ourselves while the systems sustaining our problems remain untouched.

DAY 85

If there were no greed, there would be no need of armaments.
— Gandhi, *The Mind of Mahatma Gandhi*

The Buid (pronounced BOO-id), an indigenous people who reside in the Philippine Islands, are regularly cited as one of those remarkable societies who have lived peaceably with the benefit of some nonviolent aspects woven into their culture. When Thomas Gibson, a British anthropologist lived with them for two years to understand their daily life, he had a hard time getting someone to help him learn their language. Why? Because the idea of selling something, like language lessons, or even trading for it, was outlandish to them. He quickly realized that they shared everything. The only way for him to learn the language was by showing he was trustworthy and by making friends. There was no room for greed and, consequently, no need for weapons manufacturers.

Let's be "greedy" for the kind of security that comes with a strong, supportive community.

DAY 86

On Tolstoy Farm we made it a rule that the youngsters should not be asked to do what the teachers did not do.
– Gandhi, *Autobiography: The Story of My Experiments with Truth*

Gandhi felt that the best method of education for children (ok, for everyone) was through personal example. Hence, when children "misbehaved" at the ashram, he took on a fast instead of punishing them, because he felt there was something that he must have done to encourage their behavior.

When it came time to cook or to clean, both adults and children would partake in the most basic tasks, and Gandhi would join them. And so it was in the ashram's school. Teachers did not lord over students, but worked with them. Gandhi noted that this important dynamic made the students feel quite cheerful about the school. Something revolutionary was taking place: children were not learning submission to a self-appointed authority, but modeling, instead, mutuality and interconnection.

When and where does teaching begin and learning end? Is there a clear line that is crossed by age or experience? In nonviolence, there really is no clear dividing line.

DAY 87

I have come to the fundamental conclusion that if you want something really important to be done, you must not merely satisfy reason, you must move the heart also.
– Gandhi, *Young India,* October 14, 1926

Tell a smoker all the good reasons to quit smoking, show them facts and statistics, and watch what happens: nine times out of ten, they will go on smoking. The same is true of violence. From a certain perspective, violence can be understood as a form of addiction: an activity repeated so many times that the will atrophies and mere satisfaction of that craving takes over. Appeals to reason at a certain stage can have its effect, and we always want to consider the power of reason to eventually take hold. We must also, as Gandhi maintains, appeal to the "heart," the residence of the will. But the will cannot grow on its own. It requires a vision towards which to work, and an alternative to take it there.

When someone is expecting you to come at them with insults and shame, try offering them dignity and fierce compassion. They may not respond at first, and if you are using it as a mere tactic, they may not respond at all. But when it comes from the depths - when we are upholding a higher image of someone because we are not willing to give up on them, no matter what they do to us - it can have a tremendous, freeing impact.

DAY 88

I have not conceived of my mission to be that of a knight-errant wandering everywhere to help people out of difficult situations.
– Gandhi, *Harijan,* June 28, 1942

Nonviolence has little to do with other people solving our problems for us. It is about learning to address issues on our own. A good teacher of this craft will work to empower us to resolve and transform a problem, so we see a way out of further entrenching ourselves. It can be very hard and painful to chip away ingrained conditioning, but there's at least a principle to guide us: apply an opposite force or energy to counter the force coming at us. Take the challenge of terrorism. We can, to quote Noam Chomsky, "stop participating in it." That is certainly one way out of it. One further guideline could be to "conquer unkindness with kindness; greed with generosity," as the Buddha advises.

Gandhi would advise us to be proactive. There is a kind of violence that stems from passivity, and it must therefore be overcome through active pursuit. It's not a coincidence then that so many media portrayals of the heroic are fantasies of others coming to rescue us, sometimes even aliens from outer space. This is not just fictional entertainment: watch this fantasy playing out in the militarization of police forces or the growing weaponry for militias around the world, while our problems stubbornly refuse to go away. We need to get clear: no one is coming to save us. Not even unarmed peacekeepers, who we think can do just about anything, can do that. We have to work this out ourselves, each and every one of us, wherever we happen to be. Only then will we really heed the message of the Mahatma.

DAY 89

Mutual trust and mutual love are no trust and no love. The real love is to love them that hate you, to love your neighbor even though you distrust him.
– Gandhi, *Harijan*, March 3, 1946

Gandhi is a master at drawing our attention back to a single significant truth: love is a power that can be developed. If I love you only to the extent that you love me, I am not loving you but engaging in a transaction with you. If you take away some degree of "love," I withdraw that much more. That is not love, it is tit-for-tat!

Love is an open practice, not a currency, and certainly not a threat, which calculated giving certainly can be.

Gandhi inspires us to do more than we think we are capable of. He asks us to love not only those who love us back, which is easy enough, but to love those who do not even like us. Our capacity for love, closely connected to our self-respect, can grow only when we put it to the test. Nonviolence is known as love-in-action, after all, and through nonviolence we can become capable of anything, even selfless love.

DAY 90

The motive will determine the quality of the act.
– Gandhi, *Selected Writings of Mahatma Gandhi*

"Nonviolence" is a rough translation of the Sanskrit word *ahimsa,* which literally means "the negation of the desire or intent to harm." Beyond focusing on the act alone, we must look at the state of mind in which the act was carried out.

For example, a person can defend herself or others with what looks like force, but if the motive is to stop a greater harm, then, to the extent that she harbors no anger towards or fear of the opponent, her action is closer to nonviolence than violence. Conversely, it is also possible to commit an act that seems nonviolent in principle, but the state of mind behind it is violent, intending or wishing harm to the person or group to whom it is offered.

Human beings are body, mind, and spirit, so our psychological motives must factor into in how we understand ourselves and others. This is where the practice of nonviolence comes to life. We do our best to harmonize our motives with our actions, seeking to benefit others and all of life. For Gandhi, the quality of action is effectiveness in the long run, and it's a challenge worthy of us. With practice, we can actually offer resistance to others with love, not fear or hatred, in our hearts.

DAY 91

There is a law of nature that a thing can be retained by the same means by which it has been acquired.
– Gandhi, *Satyagraha in South Africa*

Some retain the impression that once nonviolence has done what they consider to be its work, they can return to using violence to uphold their victory. Gandhi would have to be a wet blanket on this idea. If something was achieved through the use of nonviolence, it could only be maintained through the ongoing process of nonviolence. Otherwise, we lose whatever we thought we have achieved. It's like reaching down into a well with a bucket, filling it, and then letting go of the rope.

Change agents in various movements have started encouraging people to look beyond any success and keep struggling forward. The movement does not stop once marriage equality is achieved, or police brutality is less common, or another gender is elected head of state. It goes on growing until everyone, literally everyone, has dignity. This journey is not a short-term commitment but a new way of life.

DAY 92

No one should dogmatize about the capacity of human nature for degradation or exaltation.
– Gandhi, *Mahatma, Vol. V*

Human beings are naturally violent. We've all heard this a time or two. It's called "innate aggression theory," the school of popular psychology claiming that human beings are innately aggressive, and, therefore, justified in violence. Professors at major universities have based courses on such a view, despite the theory being scientifically disproved, if not rigorously challenged, for decades now. Back in 1986, UNESCO hosted a forum of scientists, whose purpose was to dislodge dangerous claims and assumptions made by innate aggression theorists. In these scientists' words:

> Misuse of scientific theories and data to justify violence and war is not new but has been made since the advent of modern science. For example, the theory of evolution has been used to justify not only war, but also genocide, colonialism, and suppression of the weak.

Their statement debunks five of the most nefarious claims about human nature: that we have inherited war from our animal ancestors; that war or any violent behavior is genetically programmed; that there has been a natural selection based on our ability for warfare; that humans have a violent brain; and that war is an instinct in us.

DAY 93

The reader can have no idea of the restraint I have
to exercise from week to week in the choice of
topics and my vocabulary. It is a training for me.
– Gandhi, *Young India*, July 2, 1925

Contrary to the myth that Truth means saying everything we think is true, no matter how much it might hurt someone, Gandhi felt that Truth often required a Himalayan degree of restraint and that, strategically speaking, it was wise to work *with* people, even when disagreeing over something urgent. For some, all it takes is a word or a glance to begin an onslaught of judgment, resentment, and anger. So we insert a clever word here or a jab there to prove that we are right and the other wrong.

Gandhi, human as he was, saw this tendency in himself and confessed that he had to be extra vigilant when he wrote articles. We can be sure that when he wrote, he looked at the intention behind his words. Truth lends itself to kindness. We can turn insults around. Gandhi would often do this with a very frank but artistic, "I think you may have meant that comment as an insult, but I choose not to take it as such."

DAY 94

But I know that I have still before me a difficult path
to traverse. I must reduce myself to zero. So long as
one does not of his own free will put himself last
among his fellow creatures, there is no salvation for him.
– Gandhi, *Autobiography: The Story of My Experiments with Truth*

In many cultures around the world, people understand the idea of being "a zero" an insult. Gandhi, however, considered it an ideal to strive towards. In the same way that we talk about zeroing our impact on the climate, or leaving zero waste behind when we go on a picnic, we can aim for a kind of personal zero effect. It's not about seeing ourselves as inferior to others but rather seeing ourselves living in a balance in the world around us, whereby everyone's needs and everyone's dignity matter.

Life, work, and society are more difficult - and not a lot of fun - when we do not strive to think of the needs of others. What would happen to the world if we saw ourselves as agents of serving others rather than serving ourselves; a world where we made the radical wager that if your needs are met, then mine will count too? Gandhi hints, rather loudly, that not only would things go better, but there really is no other way to find fulfillment.

DAY 95

I want you also to grow with me.
– Gandhi, *Mahatma, Vol. 4*

When we move into conflict with someone, we can understand that we are passing through a period of growth, that through this conflict we can learn about ourselves and the relationship in question. We can see a person who is full of resentment in front of us as a person bothered by something, maybe suffering, and then we don't have to respond in kind - we can help them instead.

When hatred or resentment want to arise and take control of our hearts and minds, we can reject these feelings, strengthening our capacity to love. Our growth will naturally help the other person grow too, and our conflict begins looking like a study in solutions. In fact, we can look at that person as though we've already found a solution, as though we've already worked it out, because we know we eventually will. It doesn't mean we haven't made mistakes or have all of the answers, but it means that we are not willing to reject the person with whom we are in conflict.

Growth is not limited to personal relationships. We need to grow as a society too.

DAY 96

Experience has taught me that it is a mistake
hastily to imagine that anything that we
cannot understand is necessarily wrong.
– Gandhi, *Gandhi's Dialogue with Christianity*

Gandhi teaches us that approaching life with an open heart and an open mind is not just to make us feel good; it helps us develop our strength, security, and nonviolence. If we do not understand something, that does not make it wrong. That's easy to say, but much more difficult to uproot from ourselves.

If we lived by this single principle day in and day out in all of our relationships, imagine what we might learn. As Gandhi goes on to say, "Some things which I did not understand first have since become as clear as daylight."

DAY 97

In concrete terms, the independence should be political, economic, and moral.
– Gandhi, *Gandhi's Dialogue with Christianity*

When the flag was raised on a free India on August 15, 1947, Mahatma Gandhi was not a part of the celebrations - and he did not want to be. In many ways, the "victory" to him was hollow. Partition was taking place; India and Pakistan were being divided along a somewhat arbitrary border by an English general who had little knowledge of the culture; and tensions were rising between Hindus and Muslims. The BBC and other news outlets came to him for a statement, and he kindly but flat-out refused to say a word about the independence.

Gandhi was not easy to please as he was not satisfied with superficial changes. For him, nonviolence has to go beyond any elections. It must be fully integrated - "economically, politically, and morally" - which will, if we look at it squarely, take lifetimes (or generations, depending on your worldview). It was no small sorrow to him that so many were pacified at mere political independence, when there was more work to be done. He looked at challenges ahead, and kept right on working, escalating the work to match the escalating tensions that were ready to explode. Gandhi for a long time by then had no longer believed that politics alone could solve essential problems. But he had not lost his faith in nonviolence.

DAY 98

Means and ends are convertible terms in my philosophy of life.
– Gandhi, *Young India*, December 26, 1924

Where conventional thought suggests that the ends will justify the means, Gandhi emphasized the importance of the means (how we do it) over the ends (what we want to happen). He is being practical, as our means are the only thing we actually can control. Of course we must envision and hope for a certain end, but ultimately, this is never fully in our hands.

To put it another way, our means are like seeds. If we want corn, we don't plant tomatoes, we plant corn. If we want to harvest peace, we plant seeds of peace.

DAY 99

It is no easy task to restrain the fury of a people incensed by a deep sense of wrong.
– Gandhi, *Young India*, May 5, 1920

Behind every emotion is energy, and that energy is ours to harness. Gandhi, articulating one of the key dynamics of nonviolent power, knew that strong emotions had to be constructively channeled if violence was to be avoided. Doing nothing, aka being passive, could only lead to violence, because people's emotions would be running high and they would have no outlet for their anger. Gandhi promoted non-cooperation as a vital tool to "enable people to give such expression to their feelings as to compel redress."

Fast forward to today. The corporate mass media in particular tends to share stories about violence out of context, as though an event suddenly erupted and no one saw it coming. But nonviolence tells us a different story: direct violence is the result of a long process, often including structural violence, which is less visible but no less galling. Violence is not inevitable. It can be interrupted at many points with nonviolent intervention and practice before it bursts out as gunshots or fisticuffs.

Beloved community, however, is inevitable. It is just a matter of how quickly and strongly we learn to desire it.

DAY 100

I hold that, as the largest part of our time is devoted to labour for earning our bread, our children must from their infancy be taught the dignity of such labor.
– Gandhi, *Young India*, September 1, 1921

Besides character-building and local and regional languages, Gandhi's approach to education put value on the dignity inherent in the work of the hands, which he strongly felt was the driving force behind personal and political independence. Above all, he wanted students to feel that they received more than an education - they would be gifted with a vocation. He launched his educational experiments in his ashram school (beginning your experiments at home before testing them on a wider scale is a nonviolence principle called *swadeshi*).

The students felt that his first iteration of the program had an overemphasis on handicraft work. They believed they were somehow deprived of literary learning. Gandhi, in all of his experience, humbly disagreed with their assessment, maintaining that even the best schools in the world would crave the kind of handiwork education they were getting. Nonetheless, he took their feelings to heart and found a middle ground for the handicraft and literary work, namely, literary study would serve the vocational training. Reading, writing, mathematics, science - all would find a concrete context within the substance of the craft itself.

Such an education draws upon our natural curiosity and puts it hand in hand with the higher ideal of a practical purpose.

DAY 101

The foundation that Macaulay laid of education has enslaved us.
– Gandhi, *Hind Swaraj*

Thomas Babington Macaulay went to India on what was, in his eyes, a "civilizing mission" to reform their system of education. In Macaulay's own words: "We must at present do our best to form a class who may be interpreters between us and the millions whom we govern; a class of persons, Indian in blood and colour, but English in taste, in opinions, in morals, and in intellect." This is colonialism in the raw. It's cultural imperialism, another way of saying cultural *violence.*

The system in India was established to create servants for those in power under the British Raj. As a child, Gandhi was sent to such schools as Macaulay had laid out for them. Having been sent to England to study law by his family, he returned to India an English gentleman in manners but certainly not in respect to equal rights or treatment.

When Gandhi began his deconstruction of the Macauley system, he started by pointing out that mere knowledge of the sciences and literature are not the foundation of liberatory education. Real education, he maintained, was character-building. With a strong foundation of character, you consider the *purpose* of reading and writing. You will not write anything if it harms others just because someone tells you to; you become a trustee of those skills and tools, and use them for the well-being of the whole. This kind of education was "primary" to Gandhi. Whether you have a degree or not, you have dignity - nonviolence education at its core.

DAY 102

My faith in human nature is irrepressible and even under the circumstances of a most adverse character.
– Gandhi, *Young India,* January 1, 1920

For those who long for a nonviolent alternative to our educational, political, and criminal justice systems, Gandhi's words should sink in deeply. The view that we have of human nature helps us decide how to be with one another in society, and how to treat one another when we've transgressed social contracts. Human beings can transform themselves and their behaviors in positive directions - even those who have chosen violence. Gandhi's not talking about just people who've insulted us personally or who have made bad personal choices. He wants us to think broadly, to include, for example, politicians and dictators. Not that such people deserve to have the kind of power they once exercised, but we cannot deny them their basic, fundamental human worth if we want to create something else.

Approaching the world this way frees us from distrust of one another; the cultural by-product of messages from the commercial mass media, which tell us time and again that satisfaction comes from competition and peace from consuming.

Undoing our collective lack of faith in human nature will require us to unplug from such media, or at least shine a new light on its real message.

DAY 103

The best way to show how to do it, is to do it myself.
– Gandhi, *Young India*, October 23, 1924

It was Gandhi's first great campaign in India, well-portrayed in Richard Attenborough's film *Gandhi*: the indigo farmers of Champaran, Bihar state. While the farmers faced starvation and slave-labor conditions, the British landlords were in the process of increasing taxes while forbidding farmers to use their own land to grow food, forcing them to grow indigo for foreign markets. The cruelty and domination was intense. Gandhi went there in 1917 and spent three months taking down depositions (he was a lawyer, remember), defying orders for him to leave the district.

Gandhi explained to two prominent leaders from the region that they might have to face loss of property, other setbacks, and jail. "We're willing to face everything else," they said, "but not jail." As they were leaving, they stopped and looked at each other: here's this man who's not even from the district and he's willing to go to jail - and we're not? Sheepishly, they went back in and said they were willing to do that too. "Then victory is ours!" Gandhi called out.

Gandhi was not the kind of person who would recommend that others do something he was not willing to do himself. In nonviolent leadership, there's a willingness to share in the consequences of an action.

DAY 104

None can be born untouchable, as all are sparks
of one and the same fire.
– Gandhi, *From Yeravda Mandir*

In working to free India from external oppression, Gandhi also dedicated himself to reforming Indian culture itself, particularly "untouchability," the doctrine that denies some people by birth a place within the Hindu caste system, forbidding them, for instance, to enter certain temples or eat with "caste Hindus." The issue continues to inspire ongoing efforts to uproot it (the class known as "untouchables" in Gandhi's day have chosen to call themselves Dalits, or the oppressed, to stress the point).

Though Gandhi did not seek to immediately undo the caste system, research strongly suggests that he was going in that direction. It appears his overall goal was to end caste strategically, by influencing people to change their consciousness, where the seeds of "otherness" germinate. We cannot condemn Hinduism alone for this problem.

Sadly, there is the concept of "outcast" in every culture and religion. In every society, we continue to perpetuate the false belief that by wealth, skin privilege, nationality, and so on some lives matter more than others. While we must work to put protective laws in place to keep such violence from being legal, we must also work to change our consciousness around the existence of the "other." As wisdom traditions uphold, in our beautiful and healthily diverse human family, there can be no "other."

DAY 105

Nonviolence is the greatest force at the disposal of humankind.
– Gandhi, *Harijan*, July 20 1931

Whenever anyone tries to say that violence works better than nonviolence, we like to tell them the story of Antoinette Tuff. Working as a bookkeeper in a public school in Decatur, Georgia, Tuff had no special training in nonviolence, but she single-handedly managed to disarm a young man who entered the school with loaded weapons. How did she do it? By expressing empathy and love - and doing so fearlessly. By humanizing someone who was already so dehumanized that he was prepared to take the lives of others and himself.

Gandhi was not a man prone to exaggeration. By 1931, when he made the above claim, he had been experimenting in the science of nonviolence for close to forty years. Each day, his earnest search revealed new insights, new discoveries. And he was not conducting mere thought-experiments, as a philosopher. His discoveries were earned, we might say, while he engaged in a great struggle to overcome the world's mightiest empire of his time - without firing a shot. So when he says that nonviolence is "the greatest force at the disposal of humankind," we should really give weight to it.

DAY 106

It must be taken for granted, that when civil disobedience is started, my arrest is a certainty. It is, therefore, necessary to consider what should be done when the event takes place.
– Gandhi, *Young India,* February 27, 1930

Preparing months in advance for the great Salt March, Gandhi asked those in the movement to think about what would happen when - not if - he was arrested. The movement should keep on going, thus defeating the whole point of arresting him! Mostly, it should have a strategic plan for moving forward all the more strongly, where his jailing would become the sign of escalating to another action. Gandhi went on to suggest these three choices to the satyagrahis: 1. prison, 2. civil disobedience, or 3. the spinning wheel (or some other constructive work to advance independence).

How often do we remember to plan ahead like this? We have seen the pattern of a dramatic action for a person to court arrest, then activists try to get that person media attention and/or out of jail. It's a very scripted process, and somewhat stunted in the big picture. So, what if we had another plan under our belts, and let the arrest be a sign to take the struggle to the next level? Expect arrest - let the movement's key figure be arrested, and stay arrested, and yet, keep the civil disobedience going, maybe at a more intense level. The constructive program, too, could take on a new dimension. Activism would be reignited.

DAY 107

Khadi has been conceived as the foundation and the image of ahimsa. A real khadi wearer will not utter an untruth. A realkhadi wearer will harbour no violence, no deceit, no impurity.
– Gandhi, *Mahatma Vol. 4*

Gandhi was a genius at using simple ideas, such as taking household items everyone could relate to and turning them into a focus for human, social, and political transformation. In the case of khadi: the traditional homespun cloth became the core of a campaign to break the dependency on British cloth and rebuild India's own home industries. It was a brilliant stroke in which everyone could participate - men, women, children - and thereby build the movement dramatically.

DAY 108

Science of war leads one to dictatorship pure and simple. Science of nonviolence can alone lead one to pure democracy.
– Gandhi, *Harijan*, October 15, 1938

Rajmohan, son of Gandhi's fourth son Devdas, did not spend a significant amount of time with his grandfather as a young man, though he found each moment with the Mahatma meaningful. Rajmohan always retained a fresh outlook on some aspect of life after being around his famous grandfather.

When Gandhi would give his afternoon prayer meeting, Rajmohan would be seated next to him. These meetings were interfaith, so prayers from multiple traditions were recited - a radical act at a time when certain sects of Hindus and Muslims were escalating tensions among themselves. Sometimes, Rajmohan recalls, some angry Hindus would stand up and raise their voices against repeating the opening of the Koran. Gandhi would then ask the entire group whether the prayer should be shared, and nearly everyone would agree. Then, Gandhi would ask those in opposition to "kindly withdraw their request." Sometimes they did. When they did not, Gandhi would then say to the Hindu fundamentalists, "If we are not going to say the Muslim prayers, then we shall skip the Hindu prayers and get on with the meeting." Rajmohan felt that such instances revealed the democratic core of his grandfather's beliefs and teachings. Gandhi would not outright defy those extremist Hindus in the name of "majority rule," but he would do something to show them what they had done.

DAY 109

I may tell you that I am constantly evolving, and the application of my principles is ever widening.
– Gandhi, *Mahatma, Vol. 4*

When we first hear about nonviolence, few of us believe that it can be put to work in almost every situation and every relationship imaginable. But the seed is planted in our hearts and grow it does, even though there is always a bit of a lag time for our lives to begin to measure up to our higher ideals.

Gandhi was no exception, differing only in the degree to which he was earnest and open in his practice. He said that he came to the principle of ahimsa in the political field only when everything else he had tried through the usual legal means had failed him. He was seeking innovation for the cause of social justice, so he turned to his ancient tradition.

He began to wonder if nonviolence could not be applied in every aspect of life, if it were possible to create a culture of peace from the inside out - not only to show people a way to free themselves from political oppression but from every oppression, mental or physical. He was on fire with the principles of nonviolence, and he left his mark. Each new experiment in nonviolence changed him as well as the outside situation. As the application of his principles widened, so did his heart. So can ours.

DAY 110

We must, therefore, purge ourselves of hatred.
– Gandhi, Quit India speech, August 9, 1942

In his famous prayer St. Francis of Assisi begs, "where there is hatred, let me sow love." This line immediately follows his plea, "Lord, make me an instrument of your peace." Gandhi contextualizes these sentiments for us in nonviolent action and principle.

Hatred drives violence in the same way that compassion underlies nonviolence. The comparison (and contrast) is apt: Compassion is fierce and potent, not passive in the least. It is impossible to hate someone in thought alone - the thought itself is an action, because it has an effect on the thinker as well as the person or group of people towards whom it is directed. Likewise with compassion and love: they, too, affect the thinker as well as those who are on the receiving end of such thoughts.

It is not an insignificant detail that Gandhi would make this bold statement in 1942, after he had been experimenting with nonviolence for decades by then. It demonstrated that his understanding of the dynamics of how nonviolence works grew only more refined. As he called on the British to "quit India," he also called on Indians to "quit hatred" in their resistance to British colonialism. That was the secret to success.

DAY 111

When there is no desire for fruit, there is also no temptation for untruth or himsa.
– Gandhi, *Mahatma, Vol. 2*

When Gandhi tells us, based on his adherence to the mystical teachings of the Bhagavad Gita, to let go of the fruits of our actions, he is not suggesting that we let go of the desire for good ends to be achieved. All he is saying is that we have to take our personal interest at the expense of others out of the equation. When we see the full picture of life, we see how our own good is achieved when the wellbeing of others is secure.

DAY 112

To have a conviction that there is violence or sin in a certain course of conduct is one thing; to have the power of acting up to such a conviction is quite another.

– Gandhi, *Satyagraha in South Africa*

In the Bhagavad Gita the warrior prince Arjuna, representing you and me, asks Sri Krishna, representing supreme wisdom, "What makes me do these things?" It's a hand-wringing, agonizing question every one of us faces. Here, Gandhi is referring to the way his fear of snakes prevented him from being perfectly nonviolent to those creatures in his early days at Tolstoy Farm in South Africa. The fear of snakes runs deep for anyone growing up in India. How can we master something like that? The good news is, that's what training is all about (including direct training of the mind, for example in meditation). Years later, it was clear that Gandhi had conquered his fear. During a prayer meeting in India, a cobra slithered over his lap while he was meditating.

Everyone was horrified - except Gandhi, who calmly watched it glide its venomous way off his lap and into the forest.

DAY 113

Every village has to become a self-sufficient republic.
– Gandhi, *Harijan,* January 18, 1922

Gandhi was sure that for democracy to be possible and independence meaningful, the push had to start at the bottom, with the villages, and build up from there. With each village as a "self-sufficient republic," there would need to be work, homes, and food for everyone, because self-sufficiency is no easy task. It is one of those paradoxical ideals with interdependence at its root, since it requires everyone to pitch in.

If you want a self-sufficient, independent, and thrivingly democratic nation, such a local scale returns the power to the hands of the *demos,* or community. No one at "the top" could do anything not dictated by the multitudes below them, and their role would be to serve that voice alone.

While Gandhi was thinking about a nation like India, truly a country of villages, it's certainly applicable to our post-industrial world. You might say it's a dream, but it's certainly possible - if we are willing and ready to implement it, as, say, a parallel governmental model. Is it any surprise the contemporary systems scientist Sally Goerner confirms Gandhi's insight when she writes that "the real trick to getting bigger is to stay small and well-linked"?

DAY 114

There is not a single virtue that aims at, or is content with, the welfare of the individual alone. Conversely, there is not a single offense which does not, directly or indirectly, affect many others besides the actual offender.
– Gandhi, *Ethical Religion*

One of the most important virtues for Gandhi was self-control, or *swaraj* (*swa* - self; raj - *rule*). When we cultivate a healthy form of self-control, we grow our capacity for love and the service of those around us. We not only learn to restrain ourselves when tempted to say or do something harmful, we become more aware of other people when our fears and desires are not dictating and driving our actions, as the Bhagavad Gita says, "like some force beyond our control." In other words, when we lack self-control, we also lack a form of self-awareness - and those around us will not be unaffected.

To take a dramatic example, consider the behavior of law enforcement agents and even neighborhood watchmen killing unarmed citizens. Were they driven by fear to pull the trigger? By hatred? By a lust for power? With a greater capacity for self-control, they would know how to become aware of, and transmute, these emotions into inward courage.

Similarly, when activists take to the streets to protest such actions and they commit themselves to nonviolent discipline, they are demonstrating not only their opposition to such outbursts, but are offering an example of what a power self-control can have when we feel provoked. The effect will not be on just themselves. Since nonviolence is "soul force," its effects are not confined to one person's consciousness.

DAY 115

Religion is never opposed to economics, but is always ranged against profits.
– Gandhi, *Ashram Observances in Action*

To serve need, not greed, is foundational in Gandhi's system of economics. Such a focus allows for a system to take care of everyone. Poverty is not only degrading to the human image, as it limits our capacities on both sides of the spectrum (having too much and having too little); it is manufactured, and it can be dismantled nonviolently.

DAY 116

I refuse to suspect human nature. It will, is bound to, respond to any noble and friendly action.
– Gandhi, *Young India,* August 4, 1920

When Andrew Bott became the sixth principal in seven years at of one of the worst performing public schools in Massachusetts, he did something crazy: he fired the security staff. This was not a high school but a K-8, and yes, there were armed security staff monitoring six-year-olds! Bott did not just fire the security staff, he redirected those funds - and the "power-over" energy they represented - into a much more creative and security building apparatus: the arts.

A school where backpacks were not allowed for fear that the students would carry in weapons became "unrecognizable," in the words of one journalist. Artwork, student essays, and other creative expressions now decorate the hallway. Bott was told that he would be "killing his career" if he took this job. Far from it: Bott made one of the most meaningful moves for himself and his community.

The secret to the school's transformation has less to do with the person in charge of the school and more about the transformation he helped foster. Instead of expecting and encouraging students to live by a violent image, his new staff encouraged the young people to express themselves creatively. And what is nonviolence, at is core, if not creative energy? Imagine how such an approach changes how education can work (especially when it includes some formal courses on nonviolence in action).

DAY 117

I would like people to compete with me in my contentment.
– Gandhi, *Young India*, April 30, 1925

Nonviolence does not eschew all forms of competition. Competition can be a healthy, positive technique to help us unfold our full selves. But like anything else that can quickly become narcissistic and destructive, it has to be harnessed towards ends that benefit everyone, in which our own good is included. Ultimately, such forms of beneficial competition are not against other people. Can I be kinder than I was yesterday? Can I remember to express my gratitude faster today? Can I learn from my mistakes earlier?

Sometimes, however, we can hold up a mirror for one another, and playfully invite one another in a competitive effort that is genuinely cooperative. It's in this spirit that Gandhi throws down the nonviolent gauntlet and dares us to compete in happiness. Not the kind we see in ads where someone's mouth is wide open with excitement because they saved a few dollars on their car insurance or qualified for a new credit card. It's the kind of happiness that comes from service and a daily deepening of our capacity for nonviolence.

DAY 118

No big or swift movement can be carried on without bold risks, and life will not be worth living if it is not attended with large risks.
– Gandhi, *Young India,* December 15, 1921

Nonviolence always includes taking risks. When you get down to it, so does living, really. Avoiding meaningful risks is avoiding the nature of life itself.

Take the story of Aleksander Jevtic, a Serbian from Vukovar, an ethnically mixed town in northern Croatia. His story takes place during the bloody struggle between Serbs and Croats in November of 1991. Vukovar had just been raided by the Serbian army, who took a van full of prisoners back to a town just across the border.

In the midst of cruelties and humiliations, Jevtic was identified as a Serb by an officer who had served in the Yugoslav army with him years before. Jevtic was taken aside and asked to identify any other Serbs in the group. The officers were standing some ways back from him. He started calling out people's names and telling them to go into the room designated for the Serbs. But he was not just calling on those he knew were Serbs. He started giving Serbian names to Croats, looking at them to make sure they "got" what he was doing, sending them into the room too. People caught on, but not the guards. Jevtic stopped only when the entire room designated for Serbs was too full to take anyone else.

Jevtic was an ordinary person who took an enormous risk. Nonviolence brings these qualities out of us, in spades.

DAY 119

Leave the outward expression, the doctrine, the dogma and the form and behold the unity and oneness of spirit... Then there will be no need to divide this universe of ours between heaven and hell, no need to divide fellow-beings into virtuous and vicious, the eternally damned and the eternally saved.
– Gandhi, *Young India,* February 9, 1928

Seng Ts'an, the Third Patriarch of Ch'an Buddhism, wrote:

> Make a thousandth of an inch distinction,
> Heaven and Earth swing apart.
> If you want it to appear before your eyes,
> Cherish neither for nor against.

To see the unity of life, and help the fractured world see it, we first have to believe in it and second of all learn to see beneath the surface appearances of everything and everyone, which are and will always be, appropriately, the abode of diversity. It's also useful to "fake it 'til you make it," acting on the assumption of unity even where you've not yet seen it.

DAY 120

It is wrong to seek to escape the consequences of one's acts.
– Gandhi, *The Diary of Mahadev Desai*

Advertising tries to lure us into the mindset that consequences - be they spiritual, psychological, or physical - are problems to be solved instead of lessons to be learned. If you overeat and get a stomachache, you can take a medicine to fix it and never learn the lesson of moderation. Similarly, if in a moment of inattention you were unkind to someone, allowing yourself to be with the discomfort of the resulting situation can provide more wisdom and understanding than numbing the pain with drugs or alcohol or work.

Consciously accepting the consequences of our actions with an open heart is a path that leads to transformation. In nonviolence, we can take this lesson even further. Actively accepting the consequences of taking a certain action can prick the conscience of others. It is not for nothing that Gandhi would publicly break unjust laws and ask that the full consequence be given him. Leading by example, he encouraged others to do the same.

DAY 121

If India can discover a way of sublimating the force of violence...and turning it into constructive, peaceful ways whereby differences of interests can be liquidated, it will be a great day indeed.

– Gandhi, *Harijan*, August 31, 1947

Gandhi would often say that if a person did not have it in them to do the work of sublimation and transformation of violence, then it was better for them to be violent than passive - that is, to accept oppression, insult, or injury due to feelings of inferiority or an inability to respond adequately. Such statements were not a "carte-blanche" for violent activity. If there was violence on the part of the movement, he would call off the action, atone or offer penance, and not resume any actions until nonviolent discipline could be maintained. Gandhi always wanted nonviolence to be a choice, not a form of repression or coercion. Those in the movement willingly renounced violence to participate in what was taking place under Gandhi's leadership.

It's unfortunate now that many who do homage to Gandhi reduce his vision to a question of morality: Gandhi was nonviolent, so you must be. This kind of simplification was the last thing he wanted; he always wanted us to think for ourselves. It's a much better strategy to show people how and why Gandhi made his decisions, and let them choose on their own. People will begin to understand nonviolence in an entirely different, and more accurate, light.

DAY 122

The prayers of peace-lovers cannot go in vain.
– Gandhi, *Harijan*, February 24, 1946

Public prayer can be a powerful form of nonviolent action when used with discernment within a broader nonviolent strategy. One of Gandhi's first calls to action in India, for instance, was to strike via a national day for prayer and fasting. Fast forward to the African American freedom struggle in the 1960s, when a group of picketers saw the police coming towards them with dogs and water hoses, and instead of advancing, they sat down and prayed together. Not to mention that movement organizing took place in churches. Fast forward again to Argentina when the famous "Madres de la Plaza de Mayo" would sit in the pews, praying, while also passing notes between themselves about their movement's actions. Look over to the Philippines People Power revolution, where you have Catholic nuns praying before armed soldiers. Or go across the world to Liberia when Women for Peace organized Christian and Muslim women to come together to end a decades-long civil war. Then there was the Egyptian revolution where we saw Muslims praying while soldiers looked on, unsure of how to proceed. Or the Indigenous struggles against pipelines, fracking, and tar sands that would often include prayer ceremonies. There were the "meditation flash mobs" on Wall Street too.

DAY 123

Ahimsa is a science.
– Gandhi, *Harijan*, May 6, 1939

Modern scientific research has begun to supply the scientific foundation for some of Gandhi's core ideas. Take the discovery of mirror neurons, which neurologist Vilayanur Ramachandran calls "Gandhi neurons" because of the interconnectedness they somehow reflect somatically.

Neurons "network" with one another to transmit the electrochemical impulses that correspond to our emotional, intellectual, and spiritual experiences. A mirror neuron "fires" when one performs an action, and also when he or she sees an action performed by someone else. When you lift your arm, for example, the motor neurons that would lift our arms fire (but that's when super mirror neurons come in to tell us that only you are doing the lifting). Similarly, when we see a state of affection or an act of violence, mirror neurons live out that state or act in our own bodies. That's why it "hurts" when we see someone take a fall (and why, as neuroscientist Mario Iacoboni points out, we may think torture is something we can inflict on another but we also experience it subliminally in our own nervous system). What about when we observe someone in front of us who is afraid, or threatening, and we process that fear but override it with a secure and stable confidence? If we knew how *that* works, we'd be seeing the neural basis for nonviolence in action.

DAY 124

Those who are attracted to nonviolence, should, according to their ability and opportunity, join the experiment.
– Gandhi, *Harijan*, August 11, 1940

Gandhi's call is just as relevant today as it was then. We, too, should get involved! Explore your opportunities - the gifts you can share with the world, your abilities - and use those as tools to chip away at the dehumanization and violence casting a grim shadow over our image of ourselves and our relationship to the world around us.

Unlike training soldiers for violence, where we brainwash people into wanting to harm others and repress any sense of independent thinking that might awaken a sense of responsibility for their actions, Gandhi wants us to draw upon our deep, inner voice and act on it with full consciousness of our responsibility. He is not asking us to do anything beyond our capability. He asks us to make our best contribution. That is not to say, however, that we can be complacent, because this kind of work is a tool for growth. We will learn to face new challenges and answer new calls to action. No one need feel left out. There is room for everyone, and Gandhi is inviting us in.

DAY 125

I want to realize brotherhood and identify not merely with the beings called human, but I want to realize and identify with all life, even with such beings that crawl on the earth.
– Gandhi, *Mahatma, Vol. 2*

In reading these words from Gandhi, we can't help but to think of Arne Naess, the Norwegian philosopher and environmentalist who is credited with coining the term "deep ecology." Particularly because Naess is regarded to a certain degree as someone attempting to draw from Gandhi's example in simplicity, nonviolence, and reverence for life.

Deep ecology is an indigenous-inspired form of evidence-based systems thinking that shows that life is an interconnected web. Life is a delicate balance, where the extinction of one species due to human causes can upset the wellbeing of an entire ecosystem, returning to bear upon human survival as well.

Naess discusses what this balance looks like in practice, and he takes the example of finding venomous snakes near a children's playground. Should we not get rid of the snakes to protect the lives of the children? His answer was certainly, and Gandhi would agree. But Naes goes further: We have to ask ourselves why we would build a playground in an area where there could be venomous snakes in the first place. Snakes have a right to life as much as we do, and it is important to familiarize ourselves with the ecosystems in which we live and play. The more we know, the better we can decide how to maintain and preserve balance.

DAY 126

I am not a visionary. I claim to be a practical idealist.
– Gandhi, *Young India,* August 21, 1920

Idealism is a beautiful state of mind, a vision of possibility of what could be. But it can be naive, and even destructive, if it is not coupled with the means for putting it into practice. To paraphrase Martin Luther King, Jr., love without power is soft and weak, and power without love is reckless.

Nonviolence is the combination of both love and power, or as Gandhi called it, "practical idealism." What could be more practical, anyway, than finding a way through conflict without harming anyone in the process?

DAY 127

Ahimsa means the eradication of the desire
to injure or to kill.
– Gandhi, *The Collected Works of Mahatma Gandhi*

A-hiṃsā is most probably what linguists call a desiderative based on the root *√han,* "injure, strike, slay" - the desire to injure. Gandhi's use of ahimsa illustrates how his principled nonviolence was located in the heart, or at least in the mind. Others who had not reached the depth of commitment in which one wishes one's opponent well even while struggling against his or her injustice could, nonetheless, partake in a largely principled movement, what he called the "nonviolence of the brave," if they clove to his lead. We often say today that it's not necessary to have a mahatma to practice nonviolence and build campaigns on it. That's no doubt true, but having one would sure be nice!

DAY 128

If national life becomes so perfect as to become self-regulated, no representation becomes necessary.
– Gandhi, *Young India*, July 2, 1931

Gandhi's ideal political system, in two words? Enlightened anarchy. If you're like us, you may need a moment to take that in...

Gandhi insisted on swaraj, or freedom. When he spoke about freedom, he meant much more than freedom from the British Raj through self-sufficiency and economic independence. He was also talking about a society where each person had enough nonviolent discipline to be able to look as deeply inward at themselves as they look out to the world in which they wish to live. He puts it this way: "In such a state everyone is his own ruler," and then he goes on to say, "In the ideal state therefore, there is no political power because there is no State." And then he adds, whetting our appetites even more, that in such a state there wouldn't be any need for police and military. Then he comes back to Earth a bit and reminds us that this kind of state is an ideal, like perfect ahimsa. As with all ideals, all we can do is strive towards them. That struggle is worth every ounce of energy we give.

The way forward, then? Develop the mindset of personal swaraj by developing these ideal qualities within ourselves. As we often like to say, nonviolence is not about putting the right kind of person in power but about awakening the right kind of power in people.

DAY 129

Yajña is not yajña if one feels it to be burdensome or annoying.
– Gandhi, *From Yervada Mandir*

Yajña is the Sanskrit term for sacrifice or offering, and every faith includes yajña. Muslims offer yajña yearly during the month-long fast of Ramadan. Catholics offer yajña during the season of Lent. A yajña is not limited to formal worship. We can make every moment an offering when we keep our eyes focused on a goal like nonviolence. The food we eat; the work we do; the words we use; the way we greet neighbors; the thoughts we focus on: all can be done in a spirit of love and sacrifice.

Gandhi gives us valuable insight into our own experiments in daily acts of nonviolence and in making our lives an offering: We must do it cheerfully, because the real renunciation, or 128ajna, is of our mental attachment to our likes and dislikes. The minute we complain that we are not up to it, or feel it to be a burden, 128ajna loses its power.

DAY 130

You may not waste a grain of rice or a scrap of paper,
and similarly a minute of your time. It is not ours.
It belongs to the nation and we are trustees of it.
– Gandhi, *Young India,* March 19, 1925

Gandhi was quite fond of trusteeship, a concept he borrowed from English civil law. Trusteeship replaces ownership and possession, the cause of so much conflict, with duty and responsibility. If you have access to anything, or if you are possibly its "owner" in the eyes of the law, it is your duty to use it for the good of society - and to get the full spiritual benefit, not to think of it as "yours" (*aparigraha*, or not grasping, was one of the spiritual principles he adopted for satyagrahis).

In the above quote, Gandhi is talking with "inmates" of his ashram ("inmates" was used to describe those who live in a spiritual community!), who have chosen to lead a simple life based on nonviolence to develop themselves, not just for personal gain but to engage in the Free India struggle. Hence their day-to-day practice consisted of becoming aware that they were working for the good of the whole, in which their own good was included. As trustees of such a mission, Gandhi emphasized, they should not waste a thing. Not a grain of rice, not a scrap of paper, not a minute of their time. Behind every grain of rice is the work of a farmer, whose wellbeing is included in the struggle. Behind every piece of paper is a part of nature, whose wellbeing is a part of the struggle. Behind every minute, there is a choice - to live for oneself or to live for others.

Imagine what an impact such an attitude change would have on our economy, our environment, and our spiritual development today.

DAY 131

The principle idea is to impart the whole education
of the body and mind and the soul through the
handicraft that is taught to the children.
– Gandhi, Harijan, June, 11, 1938

The *takli* is a little handheld spindle with ancient origins. It is not quite what is known as a drop spindle, the kind you connect with a piece of fiber and let drop while it adds twist to a yarn. The takli is more like a puzzle. First you connect your fiber and draw out some yarn from the raw material, carefully so it won't break. Then, you twist it and pull upward at an angle to add more twist (twist gives a yarn its strength). As Gandhi revived the spinning wheel, he also revived its ancestor the takli, for which he had the utmost respect. Put a pencil in your hand and quickly spin it around with your fingers for a while to get an idea of the hand "workout" that using the takli provides.

Gandhi's ideal form of *nai talim,* or new education, would put the takli into the hands of children, teaching them to spin cotton from a humble tool. They would learn of its origins, why it fell into disuse, and even get a course in the exploitation of India by the East India Company. These lessons would awaken their relationship with their ancestors as well as the spiritual values of ancient India in a way that would whet their desire for working towards Independence.

DAY 132

There come to us moments in life when about some things we need no proof from without. A little voice within us tells us, "You are on the right track, move neither to your left nor right, but keep to the straight and narrow way."
– Gandhi, *The Leader,* December 25, 1916

We sometimes have no outward reason to offer nonviolence. Perhaps people around you are encouraging you to respond to a violent situation in kind, yet as nonviolence practitioners, we still refrain and offer dignity. The motivation for nonviolence comes from within. While you don't necessarily see an outward change in someone who is offered nonviolence, you are not convinced to give up - you know that inwardly, within yourself and that person, something is taking place.

It's because we have such a narrow view of who we are, that we tend to ignore what goes on within us. We can change that by expanding our definition of who we are as human beings. As mind, body, and spirit we are privy to a greater knowledge of the workings of the great law of love, as Gandhi called nonviolence.

DAY 133

The truth is that power resides in the people
and it is entrusted for the time being in
those whom they may choose as their representatives.
– Gandhi, *Mahatma, Vol. VI*

"Shared power" is a basic concept that encapsulates the dramatic shift that must occur with a nonviolent approach to organizations and leadership. Sharing power does not necessarily change the forms and structures already in place, but it does change the conscious dynamic within those structures.

Take a lecture by an expert, in which many people in the audience hold expertise of their own. A "power-over" model might designate the speaker as the most powerful person in the room. We could be under the impression that the dominant perception in the room disregards those around us in favor of a talking head. But looked at through the eyes of shared power, we might see how the audience is empowering the speaker to share her gift. The structure may look hierarchical, but beneath the surface, a horizontal and cooperative dynamic can exist.

Sometimes we are the ones who are being lifted up, and sometimes we are among those who do the lifting. Either way, we never forget that the person we are lifting depends on our holding them up. If they abuse the opportunity to which they were entrusted, we simply bring them back down, and in the spirit of restorative justice, we might tell them they can try again when they are ready.

DAY 134

I do not love you because you agree to love me.
I love you because I feel it is my duty to love you.
– Gandhi, *Day to Day with Gandhi, Vol. 4*

All of us are subject to someone not liking us at some point, whether we think we deserve it or not, whether we like the person who does not like us, or whether we even know them. Someone else's state of mind need not affect our own. If someone doesn't like you, that's not the time to move away from them, even if everything inside says to let them have it. Instead, that's the time to move closer to them. Try to find common ground. This, he reinforces, is learning the true meaning of love, and the real grit of nonviolence. Gandhi was a master at this skill.

What happens to love when we see it as a duty instead of a contract? It's no longer a question of how much you love me; instead, it becomes whether I have done everything I can to show you kindness, compassion, and concern. No amount of ill-will directed at us personally should ever diminish our capacity for accessing those human responses. No one can be loved by everyone, but all of us can learn to love everyone. This is the way of nonviolence, of love, of the truly brave.

DAY 135

The silent cry goes out daily to help me to remove
these weaknesses and imperfections of mine.
– Gandhi, *Harijan*, June 22, 1935

For nonviolence to work at its full capacity, we have to let it pass through us, without getting in its way. Maybe because of something that happened to us in our past, we find it hard to forgive others. Perhaps we have insecurities about ourselves, so we cast judgment and blame on others. All this can block the flow of nonviolence through us. This is why Gandhi called nonviolence a "two-edged sword" (yes, he allowed himself that simile): to really use it, we have to set about transforming our weaknesses, which in Indian philosophy are called *samskaras*, or the tendencies that have become deeply ingrained through repetition.

Nonviolence engages our whole self: mind, body, and spirit. If it seems that nonviolence doesn't work, we can ask, as Gandhi did, how we can change our own hearts and figure out how we could have made it work more effectively. Not realizing this, many an activist has thrown it away after trying it once or twice without the hoped-for success.

Nonviolence is like a current of electricity, and Gandhi realized that he
was not the "doer" but a channel.

DAY 136

We often make terrible mistakes by copying bad examples.
– Gandhi, *Young India*, February 16, 1921

New activists tend to copy tactics that have been used by others, without seeing the strategy those tactics were meant to enact. Unfortunately, this inability to understand strategy is often due to a lack of one. Whenever we act without a strategy, we might do our goals a disservice and weaken other movements that would try to copy our actions in turn.

The Occupy Movement, for instance, did not have an overarching, long-term strategy. Occupying public spaces is a tactic. We're not saying that Occupy didn't accomplish anything; not at all. But imitation can't keep a movement going for long, as we saw. Only a strategy based on principled action can do that.

Without context and strategy, an action will garner attention for the spectacular tactic but not the issue. Instead of copying tactics, we can take the time to learn from other movements, whether successful or not. What could they have done with a clearly articulated strategy? If they did have a strategy in place, when did they escalate?

We can also develop and spell out our own strategies: This is what we are doing, and this is how we are doing it; these are our principles; this is our Plan B and C. And we can give people a way to opt in and maintain nonviolent discipline when they join us.

DAY 137

If I had no sense of humor, I should long ago have committed suicide.
– Gandhi, *Young India,* August 18, 1921

When Gandhi arrived in Marseille on his way to the Second Round Table Conference, he was wearing his traditional Indian clothing, a dhoti and shawl. According to one biographer, his apparel "scandalized the French journalists." In going through customs, Gandhi declared: "My earthly possessions consist of six spinning wheels, prison dishes, a can of goat's milk, six homespun loincloths and towels, and my reputation which cannot be worth much." In the midst of serious times, his sense of humor disarmed people and drew them to him naturally.

Gandhi didn't just use gentle humor with people who were inoffensive to him but to those who were unkind or disrespectful as well. He showed us that humor can be used gently, and with discernment, and need not be a tool to hurt, humiliate, or isolate people.

DAY 138

I for one will not hesitate to give water or food
to a soldier who comes to me with hands
red with murder.
– Gandhi, *Mahatma, Vol. 6*

Gandhi understood that nonviolence was the active and radical expression of empathy. There was no one, in his book, who did not deserve kindness, respect, and access to the goods that meet basic human needs.

So when someone accused him of supporting the British war when he okayed the sale of khadi blankets to the British military, he stood behind his decision, stating that it was "not proper" for him to inquire "whether the blankets were for the use of soldiers or for someone else."

It would be a different case altogether, he went on, if they were buying poison or some kind of weapons. In that case, the seller has every right to ask for more information in regard to the purchase, but not blankets, food, or water. The reason? "My humanity would not let me do otherwise." He then welcomed disagreement: "If you think that a nonviolent man may not sell rice or blankets to soldiers, then you are welcome to your interpretation of nonviolence."

How to enact nonviolence can be subject to interpretation, and Gandhi did not seek to make it an ideology, a stick used to beat someone into submission. It's an open hand, an invitation to take what you need and leave what you do not. Supporting human needs is always a peace effort.

DAY 139

A mere belief in ahimsa or the charkha will not do.
It should be intelligent and creative.
– Gandhi, *Harijan,* July 21, 1940

Once when asked about Hitler, Gandhi said we should look seriously at the efforts he was putting forward. We have to work hard to concoct the violent world we have today. The dictator did not merely believe in destruction, he acted on it with intense attention and innovation, probably not thinking of anything else. Yet he was not invincible. If one person can do that much violence, Gandhi wanted us to imagine what one - or all of us - could do with nonviolence. But it will not work if we only believe in it or hope it will prevail. It requires our total attention, the sum of all our energy. It must, as Gandhi said, "be intelligent and creative": not merely a reaction when something is not going right, but a program for forward movement so violent leaders cannot take us where they want to go.

In the same way that terrorists recruit and strategize today, the world-wide nonviolent movement must do the same. Draw people away from violent means and be proactive. Offer campaigns, start new collaborations, grow new institutions. Dream of the world that could be possible, and never stop working until that dream is realized. Be consumed by it. Anything so precious requires earnest striving. Why would it come easily?

DAY 140

People who believe in the simple truths I have laid down can only propagate them by living them.
– Gandhi, *Mahatma, Vol. IV*

Wouldn't it be wonderful if you could learn about love by reading a play by Shakespeare, instead of living through the pain of loving someone who can't or won't love you back? Wouldn't it be easy if we could get everything we needed to develop our nonviolence by quoting the great peacemakers at length, without ever needing to hold back a single impulse toward greed or resentment? But it doesn't work that way.

Learning wisdom-in-action involves more than intellectual capacities. The intellect is a helpful tool, though ultimately knowledge must reach the heart. It must, in other words, become seamlessly woven into our thoughts, words, and actions as a natural given.

In nonviolence, we search our experiences and let them speak to us. Did that harsh word increase or reduce suffering? Did I feel happy when the person I love experienced something they enjoyed? Then with the help of the intellect, we can analyze our experiences and ask, for example, how to expand this reality to inform institution-building and social movements.

DAY 141

I have not the shadow of a doubt that any man or woman can achieve what I have, if he or she would make the same effort and cultivate the same hope and faith.
– Gandhi, *Harijan*, October 3, 1936

Anyone. Nonviolence is not reserved for those who have been good all year long, were born into families with "hippie parents," or were raised in India. Even Gandhi himself did not start out with a silver "spiritual spoon" in his mouth. He made mistakes. He had to work at it every day, but every day was new to him and a new chance to grow closer to the goal.

Nonviolence is not beyond our reach, he assures us. He gives us the scientific formula to success (with the necessary adjustments for our time and place): Cultivate the same hope and faith he has, then combine that with his same level of effort.

Given the needs of the day, could we not only meet but maybe even
surpass his efforts? There's only one way to find out...

DAY 142

Cow protection to me is one of the most wonderful phenomena in human evolution.
– Gandhi, *Harijan,* January 1, 1925

Gandhi being concerned about cow protection represented the height of nonviolence, symbolizing the protection of all non-human life. But the cow is not an irrelevant symbol, given how much human beings seem to depend on her. Even when cows die, they do not stop serving since their bones, skin, horns, intestines, and so on can be used.

Gandhi called these gentle creatures "a poem of pity," because they rely on human goodness and care for survival, and yet they cannot protest against the demands that humans place on them, "expecting nothing but grass and grain in return." To Gandhi, "The appeal of the lower order of creation" is "all the more forcible because it is speechless."

All creatures can benefit from our increased sensitivity to the forces of consciousness that pervade all of life, which we come to know more fully through the daily practice of nonviolence.

DAY 143

True art takes note not merely of form but also
of what lies behind.
– Gandhi, *The Mind of Mahatma Gandhi*

The word "nonviolence" can sometimes conjure up notions of austerity and discipline. But the purpose of discipline is to get still enough to perceive how the world is a work of art. Every tree and every cloud, every canyon and river, and the creatures living therein: all are artistic expressions of an underlying creative principle.

There is beauty everywhere, in every part of life. Gandhi asks us to see not just the form "but what lies behind" the form. When we contemplate the processes that make life possible - the biological, evolutionary, and spiritual - we can orient our perspective to seeing ourselves as a part of this great art, and that same creative power that lies behind all of life.

DAY 144

Man is both matter and spirit, each acting on and affecting the other.
– Gandhi, *The Mind of Mahatma Gandhi*

Gandhi saw humanity, and life in general, as more than meets the eye. A vision like this cannot but express itself in nonviolent action. The more expansive a notion we have of ourselves as interconnected with the rest of life, the more powerfully we can move in the world, because we are moving with our full selves present and honored, and honoring and making room for others in the same way.

DAY 145

I cannot attain freedom by a mechanical refusal to act, but only by intelligent action in a detached manner.
—Gandhi, *Young India*, September 17, 1921

Gandhi read the Bhagavad Gita every day. This spiritual classic tells the story of a warrior, Arjuna, and his mentor, Krishna. Krishna, for what it's worth, is only taking the form as a dear friend, for in reality, he is a God. Arjuna finds himself in the midst of a war and loses courage. He turns to Krishna for advice, and in their conversation, Krishna reveals to Arjuna the secret of life. Krishna also grants him the supreme vision of life as a whole, not through the intellect but with an overwhelming vision that draws upon every sense and strength of the human being.

Gandhi was convinced that the Gita was not about an actual war but rather the tale of the inner struggle we all must face as we search for true freedom (not just freedom from others, but freedom from ourselves). He describes the theory of action laid forward in the Gita when he states that freedom can only be attained through detached action. The *Gita's* Theory of Action can be summed up as: use the right means, in a just cause, and let go of the results. This is the nonviolent way to freedom.

DAY 146

Ill-digested principles are, if anything, worse than ill-digested food.
– Gandhi, *Mahatma, Vol. 4*

Food is to the body what principles are to the spirit. When food is rotten, it can harm the body; when our principles are corrupted, they harm us and conceivably the world around us. Thus Gandhi maintains that harm to the spirit is worse than harm to the body, because the body is more easily healed and repaired.

Most of the world's justice systems are a prime example of two poorly understood principles: peace and security. Until we let these principles sink in deeply enough on a collective scale, we will continue to isolate humans who have already been alienated; we will continue to murder human beings for murdering others or drop bombs on human beings who are already victimized by their own governments. Such actions only perpetuate cycles of massive insecurity and agitation.

If we wonder why there is war and violence, we just have to look to where our principles stop short of including everyone. At the same time, we might conjecture that "well-digested" principles are the compost that helps individuals and society grow to their fullest.

DAY 147

We have instances in history where terrorism has failed to impose the terrorist's will upon his victim.
– Gandhi, *Young India*, June 9, 1920

The September 11, 2001 terrorist attacks led the United States into two wars, while xenophobia and Islamophobia in the country grew alarmingly. Those who provoked the violence had won - they achieved the effect of furthering violence - while the American people lost.

Gandhi maintains that there are instances when terrorism fails to provoke further violence. Take the example of Malala Yousafzai. When the Taliban shot her in the head, she met the effort to silence her by using her voice for nonviolence:

> They thought that the bullets would silence us, but they failed. And out of that silence came thousands of voices. The terrorists thought they would change my aims and stop my ambitions. But nothing changed in my life except this: weakness, fear, and hopelessness died. Strength, power, and courage was born. ... This is the philosophy of nonviolence that I have learned from Gandhi, Bacha Khan, and Mother Teresa. And this is the forgiveness that I have learned from my father and from my mother. This is what my soul is telling me: be peaceful and love everyone.

Even with the extreme provocation of terrorist violence, we need not be compelled to respond back with violence ourselves.

DAY 148

Not to think badly of anyone, not to wish ill to him though we have suffered at his hands, not to hurt him even in thought, this is an uphill task, but therein lies the acid test of nonviolence.
– Gandhi, *Ashram Observances in Action*

As a boy, Gandhi stole money from a woman who worked in his home to buy, of all things, cigarettes. Later, one key vow of Gandhi's ashrams was *aparigraha,* or non-stealing (also called non-grasping). It leads to simplicity: the more extravagant our lives, the more we take, just to have more.

He also drew out aparigraha relating to actual thieving in the ashram, by visitors as well as residents. His policy was not to punish those who stole. "We do not call the police; we put up with the losses as best we may." He recounts the story of a visitor-thief being caught red-handed and bound up by a resident. When Gandhi learned what happened, he freed the man. "Ahimsa demands more of us than this," he said. "We must find out and apply methods which would put a stop to thieving all together."

His plan comprised several layers. The first was to reduce the amount of possessions one had, so as not to tempt others with them. Another was to work with surrounding villages for economic uplift and reform. Finally, the ashram should ensure that everyone felt a sense of belonging there.

As always, Gandhi was going for the long-term solution.

DAY 149

It is not literacy or learning which makes a man,
but education for real life.
– Gandhi, *Harijan*, February 2, 1947

Education has undergone a dramatic shift in recent decades. Where it once served to expand the mind, it has become a tool to expand the wallet and the ego. An education seems to be worth less if there is not a paying job on the other end of it, a change effected without discussion and by all parts of the political spectrum. With the high cost of education, getting a job at the end makes undeniable sense. But let us also point out that when a system disempowers you for years by leaving you with the impression that the only thing you can do with your life is finance it, and by other structures and ideas within modern education, you will come out seeking power.

Gandhi encourages us to ask what needs our society has, and to direct education towards those ends. Wealth and power over others are not our society's needs. Housing is our need. So we should educate people to build eco-friendly houses. Food is our need; teach people to grow healthy food. Bonding is a need; teach people how to work together for the wellbeing of all. Meeting our needs like this would allow us to flourish and re-establish the purpose of education.

DAY 150

Human nature will only find itself when it fully realizes
that to be human it has to cease to be brutal.
– Gandhi, *Harijan,* October 8, 1938

Masculinity and violence tend to be conflated, with "manly" often meaning shutting oneself off from one's emotional awareness, committing violence on other creatures, or exploiting the earth's resources. Of course it includes the violence in wars run mostly by men who do enormous harm to other people in other lands, often only to get rich. If we are to change the story of violence, we need to change the story of what it means to be a man as well as a human being in general.

Those around Gandhi did not tend to look at him as either male or female. In his search for the full realization of his human nature, he became a balanced blend of masculine and feminine qualities. One of his nieces, Manubehn, wrote a short book about her time with her famous uncle called *Bapu - My Mother*. "Bapu" means father, but Gandhi was less like a father to her than a nurturing parent, embodying both Father and Mother.

Imagine if our definition of manliness were to lose the connotation of violence; if our understanding of what it means to be human illustrated a harmonious blend of masculinity and femininity. Human: neither passive nor aggressive, but nonviolent.

DAY 151

I take up my task of leading you in this struggle,
not as your commander, not as your controller,
but as the humble servant of you all.
– Gandhi, *Press Report*, August 8, 1942

There is a saying about leadership in *The Gospel of Sri Ramakrishna*: "Everyone wants to be the teacher; no one wants to be the disciple." Gandhi turned this around: the greatest leader would serve others and work for everyone's benefit - not seeking power, but releasing it for the whole. That is the essence of service.

It is a sacred realization when we begin on the path of asking ourselves, How can I use my dearest possession - my life - to raise up others, instead of trying to step on others on my way to the top? Lao Tzu, the founder of Taoism and author of the *Tao Te Ching*, describes this state beautifully: "The sage stays behind, thus he is ahead. He is detached, thus at one with all. Through selfless action, he attains fulfillment."

DAY 152

I must strive my utmost, during the coming year of grace, to express in every little act of mine whatever love I am capable of.
– Gandhi, *Young India*, October 23, 1924

One of the most interesting things about Gandhi is the way he seems at one minute to be a political activist, with fresh ideas for strategic movement building, and the next, a yogi from the Himalayas.

What Gandhi wanted to do with satyagraha was to offer a great act of love, organized and strategic - the force of love on an enormous scale. He had the insight to see that if he wanted to live up to such a calling, he could not give short shrift to his smallest actions.

So many people claim they could never match someone like Mahatma Gandhi. But if our vision is clear, we can see that he drops bread crumbs along the path as he goes forward. He is telling us to think big, and then begin infusing our smallest actions with all of the love of which we are capable. It's about paying attention to the seemingly insignificant.

DAY 153

Patience and perseverance, if we have them, overcome mountains of difficulties.
– Gandhi, *Harijan*, May 16, 1935

Aside from *la-onf*, Arabic has two other common terms for "nonviolence," *sabr* and *sumud*, which mean, interestingly enough, "patience" and "endurance," and "perseverance." Gandhi offers us a gentle reminder of the same foundational qualities that help us pursue the nonviolent path and face the odds against us.

With patience, we are aware that it is the rare human being who will change in the blink of an eye. Transforming for the better usually requires a lengthy and highly creative process, mixed with large doses of integrity, optimism, and honesty. Gandhi would add dignity to the mix too. Very few of us actually like, or want, to change immediately, yet all of us respond to that fierce kind of patience. Perseverance means that our patience has a different quality than simply standing by and waiting for transformations to occur; we nourish them actively.

Many of us idealists expect that once we have seen into the heart of a problem or situation, everyone can see it with us ("I've changed already; why haven't you?"), and our idealism begins to slowly fade. Why should it? Remember: someone, somewhere nourished you and your vision of the world, and it transformed you. Someone, somewhere was patient with you. Maybe not everyone, but someone was, and it mattered, a lot.

DAY 154

The real rulers are the toiling millions.
– Gandhi, *Harijan*, June 15, 1947

All revolution has to begin with one strategy: change and transform our vision of what makes someone powerful.

For Gandhi, real power came from work and labor - spiritual and societal. Those who reap the fruits of others' work purely for their own gain are bound to face reality one day. Nonviolence, as Gandhi taught it, gives us the tools we need to uplift ourselves without diminishing our humanity in the process.

DAY 155

The clearest possible definition of the goal and its appreciation would fail to take us there if we do not know and utilize the means of achieving it.
– Gandhi, "Amrita Bazar Patrika," September 17, 1933

From a strategist's perspective, Gandhi emphasizes that how we achieve our goal must be as clear as the goal itself.

There's a famous conversation that Gandhi is said to have had with General Smuts, in which he told Smuts, "I'm going to win our cause," and when the surprised General somewhat patronizingly asked him how he intended to do that, Gandhi replied, "With your help." Compare that against an often heard protest slogan, "What do we want? Freedom. When do we want it? Now!"

The *when,* as in, when we want something to happen, is not the *how* we are going to make it happen. That said, a good strategist might not come up with an entire plan all at once, but she or he does know at least what to do next in the context of the larger picture. What's the moral here? Don't get carried away by visions of an ideal if there's no real plan to back it up. Or at least, help articulate the plan if it hasn't been done yet.

DAY 156

Their partiality for their own standpoint came
in the way of their giving due weight to the
arguments of their opponents.
– Gandhi, *Ashram Observances in Action*

Can we be nonviolent without listening to our opponents? Trying to hear their side is our duty in nonviolence: we want to strive for a healthy detachment from our own standpoint, especially when it is in conflict with that of others. The more we listen to our opponents with sincerity, leaving aside aggressive and judgmental motives, the more we pave the way for them to be able to hear us without feeling defensive. Gandhi would even say that it is in listening to our opponents that we can claim victory, because it is a victory over ourselves.

DAY 157

In my opinion, Rama, Rahaman, Ahuramazda, God, or Krishna are all attempts on the part of man to name that invisible force which is the greatest of all forces.
– Gandhi, *Harijan*, August 18, 1946

Gandhi was a great fan of music, especially devotional hymns. One of his favorites was "Raghupati Raghava Raja Ram," a song about Lord Rama and his partner, Sita. Gandhi added one important change to this otherwise traditional song. In the song's refrain he added the lyric "*īśvar allāh tere nām, sab ko sanmati de bhagavān,*" "Ishwar and Allah (names for God in Hinduism and Islam) are your names. Bless everyone with your wisdom, Lord."

So great was Gandhi's passion to unite Hindus and Muslims, that he brought it into an otherwise traditionally religious song. This song was then sung by the thousands who walked with Gandhi in the Salt March. Making the sacred the political: this is a deep insight into his nonviolent strategy.

In these days when so much hate and falsehood is done in the name of religion, it's striking to note how King and Gandhi made powerful use of religion for the opposite purpose.

DAY 158

God is not a power residing in the clouds.God
is an unseen power residing within us,
and nearer to us than fingernails to the flesh.
– Gandhi, *Truth is God*

In speaking thus of the radical externalization of "God" that had come to characterize most religious thinking in the West, and offering a correction that was still a bit more alive in India, orients us to the most important discovery Gandhi made and that we must make: God/Truth/Ahimsa are (or rather is) within us. Nothing can take it away from us - except our own indifference. And no one can long withstand it when we overcome our indifference, make that great discovery, and put it to use. Often we make the discovery by putting it to use.

DAY 159

Whoever tries to serve his private ends without serving others harms himself as well as the world at large. The reason is obvious.
– Gandhi, *Ashram Observances in Action*

Most of us do not grow up with the understanding that pursuing our own satisfaction and wellbeing without regard for others causes harm. "All living beings are members of one another," Gandhi said. He did not suggest that we are merely related or closely connected; he emphasized that we are not at all separate creatures. He saw all of life as a whole.

Consequently, our actions produce either good or bad effects which extend to everyone. When we begin to understand this and see it in action, we stand, at the very least, to increase in that valuable self-knowledge that makes nonviolence possible.

DAY 160

It is to me a matter of perennial satisfaction that I retain generally the affection and trust of those whose principles and policies I oppose.
– Gandhi, *Young India,* March 17, 1927

Nonviolence is a supreme art. Gandhi points to a hard-won skill: opposing someone without damaging the relationship. Indeed, in what we might call "deep" nonviolence or principled nonviolence, we are bound to become closer to those around us. Our entire lives are formed of relationships, and when we turn to nonviolence, we aim to strengthen those with ourselves, others, and the rest of life.

DAY 161

There is no time-limit for a Satyagrahi nor is there a limit to his capacity for suffering. Hence there is no such thing as defeat in Satyagraha.
– Gandhi, from the Satyagraha leaflets, No. 14, May 4, 1919

After awakening to the power of nonviolence, and refining some of its key features as a method for mass social empowerment, Gandhi left South Africa for India. It was 1914. Four years later, Nelson Mandela was born. The soil was fertile.

Drawing from the legacy of satyagraha and non-cooperation, Mandela was imprisoned in the midst of the political period known as "apartheid," which means "separateness" in Afrikaans (in nonviolence, separateness is a root of violence). Imprisonment did not convince him to end his struggle. He remained faithful to his vision of a just world, convinced that the people of South Africa deserved a more dignified existence together.

After twenty-seven years of humiliation and cruel treatment, Mandela was released from prison, at the height of the struggle to end the apartheid regime, to be greeted by cheering crowds of tens of thousands. Four years later, he became the first black President of a democratic South Africa, inspiring people around the world with his example of courage and faith. For satyagrahis like Mandela, who died in 2013, even death is not a defeat.

DAY 162

If we all discharge our duties, rights will not be
far to seek. If, leaving duties unperformed,
we run after rights, they will escape us like
a will-o-the-wisp.
– Gandhi, Young India, January 8, 1925

Gandhi is not the only one to notice that the concept of "rights" can be tricky - it runs the risk of delivering us into self-interest just when we think we are working for social justice. He even demurred at signing the Universal Declaration of Human Rights, saying he would wait for a Declaration of Human Responsibilities. Not because the struggle for human rights isn't necessary, but because if we devoted ourselves to our responsibilities, our rights would be secured and the paradigm of human relationships would be restored in the process, making it that much more difficult for anyone to take away the rights of another.

DAY 163

I do not believe that the Gita teaches violence for doing good. It is pre-eminently a description of the duel that goes on in our own hearts.
– Gandhi, *Harijan*, August 24, 1934

Many people wonder how someone who was committed to nonviolence like Gandhi could also find sustenance in the Bhagavad Gita. The story, after all, is about a war, and the warrior, Arjuna, is exhorted to go back and fight, and chooses to do so.

In all religious traditions, there are scriptures that convey their message in the form of allegory; and in all those traditions, there is a danger that they will be taken literally. Such was the dilemma faced by the author of the Gita, who used the allegory of battle for the inner struggle every one of us must undertake to realize our full potential. Conquering others leads to more violence, while conquering ourselves is the first requirement - and the final benefit - in nonviolence.

DAY 164

If even one nation were unconditionally to perform the supreme act of renunciation, many of us would see in our lifetime visible peace established on earth.

– Gandhi, *Harijan*, May 16, 1936

Instead of vying for who can have the most access to the finite resources of our planet, let's imagine a more wonderful competition: for people around the world to try to make their country the most nonviolent. Rather than building up violent armies and nuclear weapons, we would strive to create stronger legions of unarmed peacekeepers, with the most advanced training and the deepest awareness and sensitivity to the needs of others and of life in general. Who can escalate nonviolence first in a time of conflict and violence? There would be no losers in this kind of competition. And it's not unrealistic to begin such a competition, either!

DAY 165

Nothing should be taught to children by force.
– Gandhi, *Ashram Observances in Action*

Neither child nor adult learns to respect someone by being forced to do so. No outside compulsion awakens the true learner within us. All we can do is provide living examples of curiosity, wonder, and dignity.

DAY 166

Happiness has no exchange value. There's no profit from it.
– Gandhi, from *Gandhi to Vinoba,* by Lanzo del Vasto

When advertisers offer us happiness in exchange for buying something, for ourselves or others, we would do well to remember Gandhi's insight: there is no happiness outside of ourselves.

Advertisers don't really want us to be happy. Their job is to make us desire things whether we need them or not, so that we keep spending money. With that kind of exchange we may find short-lived experiences of pleasure, but not what we are actually seeking - lasting happiness, deep satisfaction. In a world of material exploitation, voluntary simplicity is a radical idea.

DAY 167

I am endeavoring to see God through service of humanity, for I know that God is neither in heaven nor down below, but in everyone.
– Gandhi, *Truth is God*

Whatever religion we profess (or don't), we all belong to the human family. Do not think about serving God, Gandhi says, think about serving those around you. Nonviolence provides the way, since violence always inflicts injury either on the person who offers it or on the person who receives it, and usually both. Conversely, nonviolence ennobles all involved.

When Mother Teresa received the Nobel Peace Prize in 1979, she humbly stood before an elite audience and spoke of the realities of the poor to whom she and her sisters had dedicated their lives. One time a man knocked on the door of the sisters' home and asked Mother Teresa to help a nearby Hindu family who were starving. She immediately put some rice in a container and headed to the house, where she found a woman and her children. The woman took the rice, divided it in two, and left as her children ate. When the woman returned, Mother Teresa asked, "Where did you go?" and she replied that she had gone to the neighbors next door, a Muslim family who were also hungry. Even while suffering from hunger, this woman was able to think of others. Mother Teresa saw this woman's action as the highest expression of love.

DAY 168

It is no nonviolence if we merely love those who love us. It is nonviolence only when we love those who hate us.
– Gandhi, *All Men Are Brothers*

Nonviolence challenges us to cleanse our heart of all resentment, bitterness, and hatred. If we merely love those who love us, as Jesus also said, how do we grow? When they stop loving us, do we have to stop loving them, then? Do we lose our capacity for love? No. We can actually grow and expand it.

By extending love to those who don't seem to really "deserve" it, we create the conditions that can help that person change. If we don't show people that higher happiness, that higher truth of love, who will? No one said nonviolence was easy. But it's the more effective way forward.

DAY 169

I have learnt through bitter experience the one supreme lesson
to conserve my anger.
– Gandhi, *Young India*, September 15, 1920

There is a period of time after something happens that shakes us up. Maybe someone said an unkind word to you. Maybe a global event - or a public reaction calling for revenge - broke your heart. That period between the feeling and our response is a very fertile, very important time. It's the key moment when we do the work of transforming an extremely potent energy into the qualities that will make nonviolence possible. Some even call this period "the nonviolent moment," because nonviolence is more than just a word that can describe an action, it's a force that is generated whenever we convert a negative drive into a constructive channel.

We might also turn to the first law of thermodynamics, which states that energy is neither created nor destroyed. It can only be transformed from one state to another. The question is whether we want to use the energy constructively, or if we want it to be used against us in destructive ways. When we understand how nonviolence works, we can begin to see possibility where before we saw only sadness, only anger. This is the magic of nonviolence.

DAY 170

Human life is a series of compromises,
and it is not always easy to achieve in
practice what one has found
to be true in theory.
– Gandhi, *Mind of Mahatma Gandhi*

Gandhi's remarkable ability to compromise often alarmed his friends, but in most cases, they eventually saw its impressive power. We gain the ability to compromise in proportion to our ability to see and hold firmly onto what's essential - usually something basic like human dignity - and realize that the rest is inessential, stamped as important only by our ego.

Because nonviolence often revolves around issues of moral significance, it is often difficult to recognize and release our hold on the inessentials. Try it, though: it's one of the most powerful skills we can develop.

DAY 171

A Satyagrahi goes to prison, not to embarrass
the authorities but to convert them by demonstrating
to them his innocence.
– Gandhi, *Harijan*, November 5, 1938

"Jail, not bail" was the cry of the student protesters during the Greensboro lunch counter sit-ins. It represents a turning point in any movement: a willingness of one or more to take on a system directly by challenging the laws it decides to enforce. But note that Gandhi makes one stipulation in regard to this tactic - do not act out of a desire to embarrass or harm anyone. When we let go of the intention to harm others, we can be of benefit to them, and perhaps even get them to change some of their harmful ideas.

DAY 172

I have, after much prayerful consideration, and after very careful examination of the Government's standpoint, pledged myself to offer Satyagraha against the Bills, and invited all men and women who think and feel with me to do likewise.

– Gandhi, in a speech made at Madras, March 18, 1919

Gandhi did not jump into satyagraha for the thrill of nonviolent struggle or for the exhilaration of meaningful action in an otherwise chaotic world. He was deliberate and conscious about his choices. He was not reacting; rather, he was responding (in this case to the infamous Rowlatt Bills), which requires detachment from oneself and a strong sense of inward security. Prayerful consideration means that we do not take on every struggle that comes along but choose wisely when to act, knowing that if we do our best to serve that cause - with conviction and commitment to nonviolence - it is bound to produce a good effect there and elsewhere.

DAY 173

Nonviolent action, without the cooperation of the heart and the head, cannot produce the desired result.
– Gandhi, *Mahatma,* Volume 5

The second time we saw Richard Attenborough's epic film *Gandhi,* it was with a peace-movement friend who turned to us after a moment or two of stunned silence at the end and said, "I had no idea he was so shrewd." There is a tendency to regard nonviolence as little more than a sentimental, nice-guy attitude - as though as long as you're kind, you don't have to be smart. Quite untrue.

Gandhi was known to quote the biblical advice that we must be as shrewd as serpents and as gentle as doves. What a pity to go through the mental and/or spiritual inner struggle to develop the nonviolent vision and then waste the great advantage it offers by not having a strategy to bring it to life outside us. (On the other hand, strategy without inner change has some, but relatively limited, effectiveness).

DAY 174

I am but a humble explorer of the science of nonviolence.
Its hidden depths sometimes stagger me just as much
as they stagger my fellow-workers.
– Gandhi, *Young India,* November 20, 1924

What laws govern nature, human interaction, the mind, the spirit, and the body? What is the nature of love? What is the most effective form and use of power, and how do we harness this knowledge skillfully? These are not poetics but concrete questions that can be hypothesized, tested, practiced, and implemented - as deeply or superficially as one would like.

There's always something fresh and new about nonviolence, because through it we expand and increase our awareness of who and what we are. It is not mere speculation: one by one, people around Gandhi attested to finding the courage and power to challenge themselves in ways that they never thought they could.

When Nai Talimist Srimati Ashadevi Aranyanayakam was asked in an interview for the film *Gandhi's India* whether she thought Gandhi took the limitations of human nature into account, she joyfully raised her hands and said, "There are no limitations to human nature."

Hypothesis or conclusion? We'll have to try it on ourselves.

DAY 175

My experience has taught me that the law of progression applies to every righteous struggle. But in the case of Satyagraha it amounts to an axiom.
– Gandhi, *Satyagraha in South Africa*

In the course of his eight-year "experiment" with developing satyagraha in South Africa (1908 to 1916), Gandhi discovered two laws. First, that if numbers of people are important in a given struggle, they will eventually be there - the cause itself will attract them. So there is no need to be unduly concerned about starting small. The second was that "unearned suffering," as Martin Luther King, Jr. put it, can awaken the opponent's conscience.

DAY 176

We want to reach not the dead level, but
unity in diversity.
– Gandhi, *From Yeravda Mandir*

The world is reawakening to the foundations of indigenous wisdom in agriculture, what some call “permaculture.” This wisdom points to diversity as the expression of a thriving, healthy system. Monocultures weaken the environment, thus reducing our security. Human beings are not separate from the environment. We’ve evolved from it, and everything that evolves from this system has an essential role to play in it. If we allow ourselves to grow with appreciation for unity in diversity among our human systems, the purpose of our evolution will reveal itself.

Nonviolence is only the beginning!

DAY 177

It is the acid test of nonviolence that in a nonviolent conflict there is no rancor left behind, and in the end the enemies are converted into friends.
– Gandhi, *Mahatma, Vol. 4*

Oddly enough, it was the British historian Arnold Toynbee who said that Gandhi "made it impossible for us to go on ruling India, but he made it possible for us to leave without rancor and without humiliation."

DAY 178

A nation which allows itself to be influenced by the fear of death cannot attain swaraj and cannot retain it if somehow attained.
– Gandhi, *Navjivan*, October 1921

Gandhi likes to challenge us, doesn't he? Here he suggests that we cannot fear death *and* achieve lasting peace and freedom. Without understanding who we are and why we are here, we become willing to harm others for one more day of security. Death is our inevitable destiny, and learning to face it, and if necessary even risk it, is our sacred duty. Its implications are not only transcendent, but global. What greater, more freeing work is there?

DAY 179

Western democracy, as it functions today, is diluted Nazism or Fascism.
– Gandhi, *Harijan*, May 18, 1940

Gandhi made this rather harsh remark in a discussion with an American friend on the topic of nonviolence and democracy. He was convinced that democracy could be saved only through nonviolence. Note the date, 1940, when there was the so-called need for Allied forces to defend the principles of democracy through violence. Gandhi, perceptive as he was, saw right through that contradiction. The full implication of what he tells us is that if war and violence were necessary to save those experiments, perhaps those experiments are not worth saving.

The less we try to defend and justify exploitation, the closer we would come to waging a real struggle to defend real democracy.

DAY 180

Interdependence is and ought to be as much the ideal of humanity as self-sufficiency.
– Gandhi, Young India, March 21, 1929

Though Gandhi's campaign in India is referred to as an "independence" movement, it was more precisely a struggle for liberation. For Gandhi, liberation - personal and social - is a matter of realizing right relationships to one another, our resources, and all of life on Earth. He clarifies that right relationships consist of two ingredients: *interdependence* and self-sufficiency.

When we aim for independence alone, we are apt to find ourselves caught up in spirals of alienation, isolation, and exploitation. Paradoxically, when we include the ideal of self-sufficiency in our understanding of interdependence, we cannot be coerced into even the best of relationships; we must enter into them in freedom.

Striking this balance is not without its challenges - interdependence is harder and takes more work, since we have to find a way to get along and be generous with others, even when we would rather not.

Gandhi was not anti-British: Liberation from the colonizers would mean establishing interdependence with them, not isolation from them.

DAY 181

The possession of anything then became a troublesome thing to me and a burden.
– Gandhi, *Young India*, April 30, 1925

When Natchiketa, the young hero from the Katha Upanishad, is sent to Death by his father, he willingly goes, curious to meet and learn from Death. Waiting for three days at Death's home (Death is out on war and disease, among other business), Natchiketa is offered three boons for his patience. He asks first of all to be reunited with his father, as they were before their conflict. He also asks to learn the fire sacrifice (the Upanishads often play their spiritual teachings off ritual). Lastly, he requests knowledge of the meaning of life - what happens when we die.

Death urges him to ask for anything else - riches, power - and not to bother with that third request, but Natchiketa won't be bought off so easily. Paraphrasing him: "How can anyone want these things knowing that you are here and you exist?" Death, who has simply been testing Natchiketa's commitment, accepts to be his teacher.

We're struck by Natchiketa's request to reunite with his father: his first priority was belonging. Gandhi affirms that belonging is more fulfilling than having belongings. He said: "As I am describing my experiences, I can say that a great burden fell off of my shoulders, and I felt that I could now walk with ease and do my work also in the service of my fellow-men with great comfort and still greater joy."

DAY 182

Power rightly exercised must sit light as a flower;
no one should feel the weight of it.
– Gandhi, *Mahatma Gandhi, The Last Phase*

If society is to learn the art of non-cooperation, education for it should begin in childhood. How often are children expected to cooperate without question, however reasonable or unreasonable the requests of adults?

We once saw a child trying to get into a car as two grown women screamed at him to wait. He couldn't have been more than nine years old. He waited, silently. Like a prisoner. The women seemed to have wanted blind obedience.

If we want children to act mercifully to one another and create a world of justice, we have to model how it works.

DAY 183

Habit is not nature.
– Gandhi, *The Gita According to Gandhi*

If our nature is good, then why do we do things that harm ourselves and others? Because there is a difference between habit and nature. We might acquire a negative habit - of judgment rather than mercy; of condemnation rather than forgiveness; of self-centeredness instead of selfless action - over time, through repeated words, thoughts, and deeds.

If we convince ourselves that our nature is selfish, it would seem to contain these qualities. But when we turn that image around, we can see our habits and tendencies more clearly and begin to do something creative to redirect them closer towards our real nature.

DAY 184

I have sacrificed no principle to gain
a political advantage.
– Gandhi, *Mind of Mahatma Gandhi*

You can always count on Gandhi for words that will soothe and refresh. In the midst of political turmoil, he is able to profess that he refuses to sacrifice his principles to gain an advantage. It's a sad commentary on the one hand: Do we take it as the natural path of politics to be loose with our deepest values? And on the other hand, it's a wonderful statement: He has an "advantage" precisely because he does not waver in his values.

Whether or not people agree with us - and whether they can or want to articulate their feelings - when we hold onto our core principles, we become stronger and more secure, because those very ideals can guide us through moments when no direction seems inviting. When we work at that level, the public conversation immediately deepens. When a popular leader speaks to those principles, people listen.

DAY 185

Just as one must learn the art of killing in the training for violence, so one must learn the art of dying in the training for nonviolence.
– Gandhi, *Harijan,* September 9, 1940

Some of the most transformative moments in nonviolence history describe people who take on the threat of death, fully consciousness of what they are doing, without lifting a finger in retaliation. Non-retaliation is an incredibly difficult form of self-restraint that requires training and discipline.

After Gandhi's arrest for picking up salt on the beach in Dandi, Sarojini Naidu led the nonviolent resisters in their Salt March to raid the Dharasana Salt Works. She pleaded: "You will be beaten but you must not resist; you must not even raise a hand to ward off blows."

Hundreds of people arrived before the Salt Works and set themselves up: some in lines to approach the entrance, others as medical assistance, and some to remind people to maintain nonviolent discipline. Journalist Webb Miller witnessed the police beating Indians with lathis. He ran away several times, unable to withstand the suffering. "Several times the leaders nearly lost control of the waiting crowd," he said. "They rushed up and down, frantically pleading with and exhorting the intensely excited men to remember Gandhi's instructions. It seemed that the unarmed throng was on the verge of launching a mass attack on the police."

The satyagrahis held firm and won India's freedom. Can you see the immense strength it must have taken not to strike back?

DAY 186

My philosophy, if I can be said to have any, excludes the possibility of harm to one's cause by outside agencies.
– Gandhi, *Harijan*, July 25, 1936

Whenever talking about the full power of nonviolence, Gandhi is sure to tell us that the first observance we must acknowledge is, the cause must be just. "Nonviolence" that aims for some political gain, seeks to humiliate one's opponents, or promotes any other form of violence would not fit that cause.

Nonviolence, when offered from the strength of conviction that comes from an unwillingness to degrade humanity or settle for short-lived gains for the few, is what Kenneth Boulding called "integrative power." Integrative power is deployed when a person says, "Do what you must, and I will not flinch from my goal." This is the kind of nonviolence Gandhi has in mind.

A cause that is just can only be harmed from within, by the actions of those who purport to be for it, because the entire universe of justice (that moral arc that Martin Luther King, Jr. spoke of) is behind it. When a cause is backed by people who are not going to be moved by attempts to foil their efforts - who have a strategy in place, and who are ready to shift and move in new directions when necessary - anything that attempts to stop them only makes them stronger.

DAY 187

I would use the most deadly weapons, if I believed that they would destroy it. I refrain only because the use of such weapons would only perpetuate the system though it may destroy its present administrators.
– Gandhi, *Young India*, March 17, 1927

It would be hard to think of a more important piece of wisdom for those of us who may be contemplating what has come to be called a "diversity of tactics," a euphemism for using "some" violence in what would otherwise be nonviolent actions. How many examples have we seen, unfortunately, of both the confusion of an otherwise nonviolent action and of getting autocrats out of power through violence only to see new regimes be installed in their place?

DAY 188

A man of faith will remain steadfast to truth,
even though the whole world might appear to be
enveloped in falsehood.
– Gandhi, *Harijan,* September 22, 1946

"Steadfastness to truth" is a near-literal translation of satyagraha from Sanskrit. We don't necessarily need to interpret faith as any specific religion or dogma. We don't need to put our faith in God to have faith in people, human nature, or the laws that govern the practice of nonviolence.

A story from the Zen tradition brings out the various dimensions of such faith. It goes like this: An armed man once came rushing into a Zen monastery and everyone went running out, afraid for their lives. One person remained inside the monastery, and that was the abbot. When the man with the sword came up to the abbot, he was incensed at the abbot's composure - he must have been thinking, after all, that a sword is power. So he said to the abbot, "Don't you know who I am? I can run this sword right through you and without blinking an eye!" The abbot calmly replied, "Don't you know who I am? I could let you run a sword right through me without blinking an eye." The aggressor put down his sword, bowed to the abbot, and left the monastery. The abbott could have been killed, but he had faith in human nature, himself, and the dynamics of nonviolence.

DAY 189

These difficulties were only passing, for the strict observance of the vow produced an inward relish distinctly more healthy, delicate and permanent.
– Gandhi, *Autobiography: The Story of My Experiments with Truth*

When Gandhi went to England to study law, his mother, who some believe was his spiritual teacher, asked him to take three vows: to abstain from women, alcohol, and meat. We could say that this is where his experiments that nourished his spiritual and personal strivings started. In his experiment with abstention from meat, for example, he was convinced by a friend that eggs should not be considered as such, and so he began to consume them. But this experiment did not last long. Gandhi became overwhelmed by the knowledge shared by his mother that eggs were meat, and it was really to her that he made his vow. So he decided that even if he could convince himself that eggs were not a meat product, he should abstain from them. He described it as a "strict observance" of the vow. Such an observance, to paraphrase, gave him a deep, permanent satisfaction.

DAY 190

All obstacles in our path will vanish, if only we observe the golden rule that we must not be impatient with those whom we may consider to be in error, but must be prepared, if need be, to suffer in our own person.
—Gandhi, *Gandhiji's Dialogue with Christianity*

While we can cultivate the means for accessing our energy at deeper and deeper levels through practices like meditation, in general we can say that the amount of energy any one person has during any given day is limited. Seething about an argument with someone, for example, would be a sure way to drain our energy from the projects that really need it.

Here we turn to the motivation: Could it be that we are driven forward by our desire to make someone less, to place ourselves above them in some way, morally or intellectually? If we want to guarantee that our interactions uplift us, it's a kind of law in nonviolence that they must uplift everyone involved, even those who are clearly in error.

DAY 191

Suspicion is of the brood of violence.
Nonviolence cannot but trust.
– Gandhi, *Young India*, May 20, 1925

Nonviolence is never about changing another person directly. It's always about changing ourselves in order to see more directly into the heart of a conflict and effect transformation there, which can, in time, change others.

We can't get to the root of conflict if our hearts and minds are agitated. We *can* get there with a higher image of others and ourselves, an image that, interestingly enough, satiates a part of our minds. Living in a state of agitation, such as of suspicion, is only possible when we hold others in low esteem or feel that we ourselves are violating some rule or law, and are therefore afraid of the consequences, whereby hatred and fear rule the day.

In nonviolence, we have to have trust in ourselves first. We have to see that whatever others offer us, we possess the inner tools to take it on. Not surprisingly, Gandhi's call to trust actually requires quite a bit of effort.

DAY 192

Ahimsa is the highest ideal. It is meant for the brave; never for the cowardly.
– Gandhi, *Mahatma, Vol. 7*

The courage spoken about here is not only the courage to face (the risk of) punishment but the scorn and disapproval of others, which can be more difficult. It is also a kind of courage to hold the faith that there is order in the universe and no good act, carried out by those without attachment to personal gain, will go without its due effect.

A conspicuous example of the second kind was when, in 1913, Gandhi held out for a real investigative commission rather than accept the stacked one "offered" by General Smuts, with its lack of Indian representatives. In holding out, Gandhi went against the advice of the viceroy, with whom he had cultivated an important and rewarding relationship, and even his revered political mentor, G.K. Gokhale. Events proved Gandhi right, and his esteem with Gokhale and the viceroy only increased.

DAY 193

I am satisfied that many Englishmen and Indian officials honestly believe that that they are administering one of the best systems devised in the world...
– Ronald Duncan, *Selected Writings of Mahatma Gandhi*

A well-known admonition of the Buddha was *na hante, na hanyate,* the wise one "will not kill, or *cause* to kill."

The famous peace researcher Johan Galtung is credited with coining the modern equivalent: "structural violence." Direct violence hurts directly, but structural violence - the injuriousness built into a structural system, such as lopsided taxation or a "poverty draft" where military enlistment is the only hope for a poor person - hurts much more in the end, and is more difficult to get rid of.

While Gandhi called the British-built governance structure of colonized India "a subtle but effective system of terrorism," many a participant was blind to what he or she was doing through it. (A bit like a drone operator for the military?) It is always dangerous when people do not, or cannot, take responsibility for their actions.

DAY 194

Those who believe in the justice of their cause
need to possess boundless patience.
– Gandhi, *Young India*, April 28, 1929

One word for nonviolence in Arabic is *sabr*, or patience. Even though Erica Chenoweth and Maria J. Stephan have statistically proven that nonviolent transitions to democracy are three times faster than armed insurrections, this fact remains controversial in social justice circles ("We cannot patiently accept injustice and patiently wait for those of us who are committing harm to change their hearts").

Gandhi is not suggesting responding to systemic injustice with passivity. Patience, rather, is the modus operandi by which we treat one another: we are impatient with systems but patient with people. The minute we treat people with impatience, we take the first step towards dehumanizing them, feeling that our cause or situation justifies using a harsh word or aggressive language.

What would happen if we did our best to be sincerely gentle with one another, as *people*, while opposing unjust *systems*? Behind this question lies the true art of nonviolence.

DAY 195

The movement...has been conceived so as to minimize
the evil wrought by the craze for amassing
large fortunes through the use of dead tools
in order to avoid having to deal with
very sensitive human tools.
– Gandhi, *Village Industries*

Gandhi saw everything he touched on - in this case, khadi and the village industry programs - as an aspect of Reality, and specifically human reality. He could take on the smallest details and the biggest picture, so to speak, in the same breath. He offers an eye-opening insight into the deadening effect of modern industrialism: how through it, people try to avoid dealing with other persons and attempt to escape into a world of dead machinery, a fatal mistake. We wage wars referring to a city of people as a "target," and we give names like Little Boy and Fat Man to atomic bombs.

While discussing a simple program of economic uplift, Gandhi has laid his finger on a flaw at the heart of modern industrial civilization. Martin Luther King, Jr. would be the first to agree: "We must rapidly begin the shift from a 'thing-oriented' civilization to a 'person-oriented' civilization."

DAY 196

The law of love could be best understood
and learned through little children.
– Gandhi, *Mind of Mahatma Gandhi*

To learn great lessons from children, we have to shift our view of who they are and what they are capable of. We cannot assume a "power-over" attitude, using coercion and punishment to have them do what we want; we have to challenge ourselves to maintain a "power-with" approach.

Children lack positive models of relationships in society. They might be raised with every luxury life can offer, but that's not enough. They need loving, caring relationships to learn empathy, trust, and nonviolence of mind, body, and spirit. If we could let ourselves see a child's full humanity, we could begin to rediscover our own. And then war anywhere, poverty anywhere, would be impossible. Let us try.

DAY 197

Man is the maker of his own destiny, and therefore
I ask you to become makers of your own destiny.
– Gandhi, *The Collected Works of Mahatma Gandhi, XXVI*

Gandhi's vision - of life, of human nature - is in so many ways an opposite and a remedy to today's popular beliefs. He is very much a prophet of what we call the "New Story."

The media tells us that we are the product of our genes, advertisers tell us that buying stuff will make us fulfilled, and some scientists still assume that evolution was a random process in a meaningless universe. Of course there is much that we cannot control, but what matters most is determined by what we think and how we live. We have to choose to become conscious agents if we're laboring under the human image in the mass media. Gandhi challenges and uplifts us by giving us back our critical agency.

DAY 198

Man is not omnipotent. He therefore serves the world best by first serving his neighbor.
– Gandhi, *Ashram Observances in Action*

We can serve others in the courtesy of everyday living, making this calling into an art. If you share a mailbox with your neighbor, why not bring them their mail? Are you going to the store? See if someone else needs something too. Is someone carrying several things at once? Ask if you can help them. With these small acts of grace woven throughout the day, we can practice seeing our own wellbeing in that of others. And then we'll be even more ready for the big stuff, like opposing them when necessary.

DAY 199

Love is not love which asks for a return.
– Gandhi, *The Collected Works of Mahatma Gandhi XIV*

Whether or not Gandhi is paraphrasing Shakespeare ("Love is not love which alters when it alteration finds," Sonnet 116), the rhetoric is common to these two experts on love - precisely because there is so much misunderstanding about love, which in a spiritual sense is the universe's root-energy.

Gandhi had to discard the definition "God is love" only because, as he said, "human love in the sense of passion could become a degrading thing also," and that begins to happen whenever we expect something in return, where our love is contractual. If there is one area where "it is more blessed to give than receive," that area is our precious capacity to give love without seeking anything for ourselves.

DAY 200

It is not that I am incapable of anger, for instance; but I succeed almost on all occasions to keep my feelings under control.
– Gandhi, *Young India,* October 1, 1931

Gandhi is not making a case for suppressing or repressing our emotions the way that men, for example, are largely taught not to show their emotions ("boys don't cry"). What he is saying is that his emotions are not in control of him. There is a space between his emotion arising and its expression. In that space, he can choose how to express the energy behind the emotion. This is a very important capacity in nonviolence.

Most people wouldn't think of Mahatma Gandhi as the angriest person of the twentieth century, but if they understood the immense power that comes from the channeling of anger, then maybe they would. Gandhi did get angry, and he directed his anger in such a way that kept it from hurting others, using it instead as a positive force for social upliftment. We can use our anger without letting it use us, too, the way fire can either burn you or light a lamp. We can let it light our own lamp and that of others who come along the same path.

DAY 201

If we had not adhered to this principle,
instead of winning, we would not only have
lost all along the line, but also forfeited the
sympathy which had been enlisted in our favor.
– Gandhi, *Satyagraha in South Africa*

Gandhi refers to one of his cherished principles in satyagraha struggles, "no fresh issue," meaning that a satyagrahi never piles on another demand just because they have gotten some leverage. That would change the dynamic of the interaction from a conversation to a power struggle. Yet, Gandhi is quick to add that "if the adversary himself creates new difficulties while the struggle is in progress, they become automatically included in it."

Satyagraha can be subtle, but it has a precise logic. The logic of love?

DAY 202

The only thing that separates us from the brute,
with which we have so much in common,
is the ability to distinguish between right and wrong.
– Gandhi, *Mahatma Vol. 4*

We can take this statement along with another that Gandhi unhesitatingly made, which is that what distinguishes us from other animals ("the brute") is the law of our being in contrast to theirs: nonviolence.

Nonviolence, in other words, is the ultimate right - or as the scriptures put it, the highest dharma. To the extent that we can carefully cultivate that critical ability to choose it, we become truly human. Our present culture, mostly delivered in our mass media, is therefore a seriously dehumanizing force; we do well to guard ourselves against it.

It may also be worth mentioning how in the last twenty or so years, behavioral scientists have systematically stripped us of every distinction we have proudly ascribed to ourselves from the "lower" creation. Our animal forebears have empathy and the ability to plan, and they make sacrifices for others. The exception is that we human beings have the ability to choose nonviolence as a matter of principle.

DAY 203

I must say that, beyond occasionally exposing me to laughter, my constitutional shyness has been no disadvantage whatever.
– Gandhi, *Autobiography: The Story of My Experiments With Truth*

If you have ever found yourself unable to speak before a group of strangers, or sat with a group of colleagues, listening intently but not sure about how to get a word in edgewise, consider yourself in the company of the young Mohandas Gandhi. To overcome his trepidation of speaking publicly, he used to prepare his thoughts in advance, writing them down. Even then, someone else would often need to read them, as he would not be able to. As he reflects on this quality of his young self, Gandhi suggests that his natural inclination towards silence facilitated his spiritual development, because a person of few words will measure each word before speaking. "It has helped me in my discernment of truth," he said.

DAY 204

This earthly existence of ours is more brittle
than the glass bangles that ladies wear.
– Gandhi, *Harijan,* February 2, 1934

When Death comes to take us, we return our bodies as dust to this beautiful earth. Nonviolence requires that we remember this reality throughout our day. Keeping the inevitability of bodily death in our minds can be difficult, but it allows us to steady our hearts on our conscious existence. *All life is a part of the whole. My life is not separate.*

Our job, as it appears, is simply giving back to life for however long we have left - and to give ourselves over to Death when it comes for us, while at the same time, never sending others in our place.

DAY 205

I believe in the sovereign rule of love
which makes no distinctions.
– Gandhi, *Young India*, May 28, 1924

There are certain human universals to which we cannot afford to lose our sensitivity. When we understand our nonviolence well and deeply enough, we should never experience a conflict between reason and heart or, for that matter, between the right and the most effective thing to do. If we have a conflict, we must be misunderstanding something. And if we can't clear it up, it's usually safer to go with heart. Reason will usually catch up, when we factor in the feedback of our experiences.

Adopt the rule of never degrading any human being. Then see what happens to our criminal justice, foreign policy, and other systems that at present operate on various kinds and degrees of degradation and abuse. When we rebuild those systems to align with this rule, voilà, we create a nonviolent world.

DAY 206

You must never despair of human nature.
– Gandhi, *Harijan*, November 5, 1938

This statement was not uttered by an overly optimistic "saint." Gandhi saw human violence: prejudice, beatings, mob killings, exploitation, starvation, you name it. But he understood that these atrocities take place because we despair our nature - when we think we are capable only of violence, we will dehumanize ourselves and others. Our capacities for nonviolence remain largely untapped. There's potential, not despair, in that realization. Despair is a luxury we cannot and must not afford.

DAY 207

> Satyagraha is a process of educating public opinion, such that it covers all the elements of society and in the end makes itself irresistible. Violence interrupts the process and prolongs the real revolution of the whole social structure.
> – Gandhi, *Harijan,* March 31, 1946

The interrupting nature of violence was true for Gandhi's time, and it is true for us today. When we keep our eyes on the goal, the "real revolution of the whole social structure," we quickly understand our need to overcome violent reactions and the dependence on violent institutions to settle our need for justice.

Our need for justice must be disciplined by the excruciatingly difficult practice of holding offenders accountable to their violence and its effects without inflicting the same violence onto them. And that's because violence affects everyone - not only those who receive it but also those who use it, even those who try to justify it in the name of a righteous cause. This is why Jesus said he desired not sacrifice, but mercy. Mercy does not hold people less accountable for their violence, yet it manages to transform people and society at a deeper level to stop such violence from happening again.

As St. Francis of Assisi said, "where there is hatred, let me sow love."

DAY 208

When a child, my nurse taught me to repeat Ramanama whenever I felt afraid or miserable, and it has been second nature with me with growing knowledge and advancing years.
– Gandhi, *Harijan*, August 17, 1934

Ramanama is the repetition of the Rama's name (Rama-nama). Rama is a Hindu deity whose story is told in the epic of the Ramayana, and the name means "joy." The repetition of a holy name or sacred word is known as a *mantram*, or prayer word, and its practice is found in all faiths. But you don't need a religion to benefit from the work of a mantram, which is to steady the mind on what is real, good, and lasting.

How immensely practical the mantram is. If, instead of reacting to fear with more fear or to anger with greater anger, we turned to a mantram to help us steady the mind and find clarity in a difficult situation, we could become more compassionate and skilled in the art of living nonviolence.

DAY 209

In this there is no room for machines that would displace human labour and that would concentrate power in a few hands.
– Gandhi, *Harijan*, July 28, 1946

It is hard to understand Gandhian Economics without the fundamental spiritual principle behind it: human beings need work. As the Bhagavad Gita says, humankind and selfless service were created at the same time. Selfless service throws a wrench into capitalist economics, which promises more down time when we turn our efforts over to machines - an illusion. Human beings rest when they feel they've made a meaningful contribution.

Gandhi is not talking about *any* kind of work, and certainly not dehumanizing work for low wages and an annual week-long vacation. He maintains that we need work that brings out our best and places human dignity front and center.

Imagine if our clothing were a local enterprise, where people learned the art and design of clothes-making. What if food, and all other household needs, were produced locally? Whatever could not be produced in small batches by local employees would be called into question: do we really need this? Selfless service along these lines would solve unemployment, and it would reignite community building.

Taking the opportunity to produce the items that we need away from us creates monopolies and dependencies - in short, violence. A nonviolent society requires calling everything into question, and our economic model really deserves a review, doesn't it?

DAY 210

Mutual tolerance is a necessity for all time
and for all races.
– Gandhi, *Mind of Mahatma Gandhi*

There could hardly be a more needed message for our day. But Gandhi will go beyond mere tolerance and argue that every child must be given a "reverential study" of all the world's major faiths. That would teach the child that her or his own faith is only one system among others, and hopefully that "He who has no respect for another religion has no respect for his own," as noted in the text of a famous edict by Emperor Ashoka, who ruled almost all of the Indian subcontinent from 268 to 232 BCE. Interestingly, Gandhi never encouraged anyone to convert to another faith, much less attempt to convert another person. He did believe that all valid paths lead to the same goal, and that being born into a particular one was not a matter of coincidence but had some karmic meaning.

DAY 211

My goal is friendship with the world and I can combine the greatest love with the greatest opposition to wrong.

— Gandhi, *Mind of Mahatma Gandhi*

When we keep the simple idea in mind that every human being has dignity, friendship with everyone is no longer hyperbole but a real (and challenging) possibility. Our dignity is our divinity. We can respect and maintain the dignity of others and retain our friendships without always agreeing with them. Even amidst great opposition to someone, we can keep our eyes fixed on their dignity - and our own. This is really Nonviolence 101: We don't have to be afraid of disagreeing when we know the respect is there. And if it works for individuals, why not for foreign policy?

DAY 212

Service and not bread becomes with us the staff of life.
We eat and drink, sleep and wake for service alone.
Such an attitude of mind brings us real happiness.
– Gandhi, *From Yeravda Mandir*

Gandhi is turning the propaganda wing of militarism, the commercial mass media, on its head by emphasizing that service - not consumption - leads to lasting happiness. But note: he understands service primarily as a mental state, suggesting that we should allow it guide us in our actions wherever we may find ourselves in the course of a day. It's not a couple of acts, in other words. Some people make a blessing over their food before taking a bite, so that the nourishment contained therein will strengthen the body and mind for serving others. How do you develop your capacity for service?

DAY 213

Nature is relentless and will have full revenge for
any such violation of her laws.
– Gandhi, *Young India*, March 12, 1925

When we violate our natural state of unity with one another, driven by our conditioned belief in separateness, we can count on the law of our highest nature to push back. "Pay attention," it says, "this is not who you are."

The basis of Gandhi's vision of nonviolence is aligning ourselves with the power of a natural law. Our efforts are significantly weakened when we go about using nonviolence as merely a means to an end - that is, believing we are separate while working to uplift a cause that arises from our unity. "Nature is relentless," Gandhi says, so we must vigilantly honor nature's highest laws in our thoughts, word, and deeds.

DAY 214

No awakening is possible without the people at large realizing their power.
– Gandhi, *Speeches and Writings of Mahatma Gandhi, Vol. 4*

Until we become aware of our power, as Gandhi encourages us to do, we are not awake but moving about the world in an unconscious state, creating the conditions for violence to spring up all around us. Even if a new person who promises to be a "people's candidate" is elected head of state, this still does not constitute personal or social awakening. When we realize we can remove a person from power through non-cooperation and direct action, that's when we know something has changed inside of us. Cultivating that consciousness, that awareness of inner security, becomes a key part of our nonviolence training.

DAY 215

The pursuit of Truth is true bhakti.
– Gandhi, *From Yeravda Mandir*

Bhakti means devotion. Kasturba Gandhi used to memorize prayers from various religious traditions. During morning prayer time, she would close her eyes and slowly recite a prayer, letting the words sink into her heart and mind. Whenever her mind would wander, she would bring her attention back to the words. Passage Meditation, which uses the technique of passage memorization and concentrated repetition, though silently. While Passage Meditation turns to the words of mystics from the world's major religious traditions - each passage points to the universal experience of union with Reality - Here is one of our favorites:

> I do dimly perceive that whilst everything around me is ever changing, ever dying, there is underlying all that change a living power that is changeless, that holds all together, that creates, dissolves, and recreates. That informing power or spirit is God, and since nothing else that I see merely through the senses can or will persist, He alone is. And is this power benevolent or malevolent? I see it as purely benevolent, for I can see that in the midst of death life persists, in the midst of untruth truth persists, in the midst of darkness light persists. Hence I gather that God is life, truth, light. He is Love. He is the supreme good.

DAY 216

The cause is great, the remedy is equally great;
let us prove worthy of them both.
– Gandhi, in a speech made at Madras, March 18, 1919

It's not enough to have a great cause. The means must also be great. Why? Because the means determine the end. Nonviolence is an ever-developing process, not an end goal. More than simply a tool for combating specific injustices, it is a "remedy," as Gandhi puts it, a way of healing ourselves, our society, and our world.

But the question remains: How exactly do we prove ourselves worthy of a great cause and the full power of a great means? In the eleventh century, the Sufi mystic Ansari of Herat said it this way: "Watch vigilantly the state of thine own mind. Love of God begins in harmlessness."

DAY 217

The humility of a satyagrahi knows no bounds. He does not let slip a single opportunity for settlement, and he does not mind if any one therefore looks upon him as timid.
– Gandhi, *Satyagraha in South Africa*

Gandhi is speaking about the tendency to get attached to something we're engaged in, therefore becoming unduly concerned about how we look and losing sight of the actual forces at play. Humility is closely connected to the ability to compromise as well as the ability to stay focused on the quest for a successful resolution - without being taken off course by a desire to "win."

DAY 218

All religions teach that two opposing forces act upon us and the human endeavor consists in a series of eternal rejections and acceptances.
– Gandhi, *Mahatma, Vol. 2*

In Judaism these two forces were called *yetsir ra* and *yetsir tov*, "the evil urge and the urge to good." St. Augustine called them "two loves" (*amores*) that are creating two social orders, the "City of Man" and the "City of God." It is our eternal capacity and privilege to choose the latter over the former at every moment. Needless to say, Gandhi's words for, and ways of looking at, these forces were violence and nonviolence. Our eternal struggle in life is to see which is which and to choose accordingly. Once we become aware of that, meaninglessness goes by the wayside.

DAY 219

The world rests upon a bedrock of satya or truth.
Asatya or untruth also means non-existent,
and satya or truth also means that which is.
If untruth does not so much as exist, its victory is out of the question.
And truth being that which is can never be destroyed.
This is the doctrine of Satyagraha in a nutshell.
– Gandhi, *Satyagraha in South Africa*

Throughout the pages of Gandhi's classic *Satyagraha in South Africa* (one of the only two full-length books he ever wrote, putting his imprisonment in the mid 1920s to good use; the other being the *Autobiography: The Story My Experiments with Truth*), lie brilliant *obiter dicta* that illustrate how he saw the Eternal shining through everything he experienced. Of all those gems, the one quoted above can be regarded as his credo. All mystics see the one positive reality behind appearances. Only a few, like Jesus, Buddha, and Gandhi, turned that vision into a world-changing force.

DAY 220

With satya and ahimsa, you can
bring the whole world to your feet.
– Gandhi, *Young India*, March 10, 1920

Gandhi loved soccer, the sport the world outside of the United States calls football. Early in his public career, (we are talking early twentieth century; he's in South Africa at this time), he started a football club (well, three, actually– one each in Johannesburg, Pretoria, and Durban). Can you guess what he called it? *The Passive Resisters.*

Did he start a sports club just for fun? Remember, his reasoning was always practical. First of all, he realized that football was the sport of "the poor" and thus a means for recruitment to the cause. Secondly, he used public matches to raise funds for the families of political prisoners while also distributing leaflets about the harm caused by racial segregation. Moreover, he liked the teamwork element in soccer. He felt it was a good form of personal training for learning skills of nonviolent cooperation. Even more exciting, though: at half-time, he would inspire his teams with talks about the principles of nonviolence. Is this the dreamiest soccer club in history, or what? Could you imagine the Passive Resisters today, offering satyagraha against things like forced evictions of the poor to build a new stadium for the World Cup? You better believe it.

DAY 221

"I am alone, how can I reach seven hundred thousand villages?"
This is the argument pride whispers to us. Start with the faith that if
you fix yourself up in one single village and succeed,
the rest will follow.
– Gandhi, *Young India,* June 17, 1926

Gandhi is giving India's idealistic students a concrete example of swadeshi, or localism. He is also providing a good example of means and ends: if you do something right, no matter how small, its positive effects will spread (and conversely, if you do something in the wrong spirit, even on a large scale, it will peter out).

We can easily succumb to despair in the face of the enormity of problems and our own (apparent) smallness. It's good to know that this situation isn't new, and that Gandhi had a solution for it, hard as it may be at first to believe it. Repeated experience and the ability to connect the dots to distant results is what builds up faith.

DAY 222

Still the community stood unmoved; only the weaklings slipped away. But even the weaklings had done their best. Let us not despise them.
— Gandhi, *Satyagraha in South Africa*

Our Mahatma tread a fine line between demanding the best of everyone around him and expressing compassion for them when they did not rise to his expectations. He held people accountable to the highest standards while being incapable of disrespect for anyone, even those who failed.

In this we can see the germ of what has become in our day "restorative justice," the approach slowly taking hold in schools and the prison system, where those who have offended take full responsibility for whatever they've done but given every chance to go forward with dignity. Indeed, it confers dignity to take responsibility; but then, as the saying goes, you are not the worst thing you ever did. Dignity was part of Gandhi's formula for drawing out people's best - and building a following that has not been seen since.

DAY 223

Even in a most perfect world, we shall fail to avoid inequalities, but we can and must avoid strife and bitterness.
– Gandhi, *Young India*, October 7, 1926

When Gandhi said this ninety years ago, he did not mean that we should put up with gross inequalities and obscene poverty. He meant that striving for leveling the outer playing field was unnecessary and largely impossible.

What we can - and must - strive for is doing away with greed and the hopeless search for happiness through material possessions. Doing so would return sufficiency to everyone. The wealthy would spontaneously shrink from exploiting the poor, and the poor would no longer feel resentment and envy of the rich.

DAY 224

I wholeheartedly detest this mad desire to destroy distance and time.
– Gandhi, *Mind of Mahatma Gandhi*

To see life as it is, and to see other people and ourselves as we are, we must slow down. Instead of enjoying long walks or journeys, we fly from one place to another or drive as fast as we can. Instead of writing letters, we text or email at all moments of the day.

Where there was room for silence and reflection, now, thanks to our technologies, we are obligated to make split decisions on everything from how we feel about your opinions to how we feel about the latest statement from a political candidate. It's hard to hear our hearts in the midst of this chaotic, incessant effort, as Gandhi said, "to destroy distance and time."

If Gandhi had patience with people who opposed him, and if he could even love and admire them, that was partly due to his efforts to slow down, at honoring both distance and time, which ironically leads to prioritizing, not neglecting, our relationships with others and our planet.

DAY 225

Let no one say that he is a follower of Gandhi. ... You are no followers but fellow students, fellow pilgrims, fellow seekers, fellow workers.
– Gandhi, *Harijan*, March 2, 1940

Leadership does not need to mean authoritarianism. Discipline does not require hierarchy. Often, it is when leadership and self/group discipline are lacking hierarchy and authoritarianism fill the vacuum. Gandhi did not say, "Do as I do." He wants us to travel the path *with* him.

DAY 226

Under the ideal conditions the barrister and the bhangi should both get the same payment.
– Gandhi, *Mahatma, Vol. 8*

A *bhangi* is a sweeper, and is placed very low in the Indian caste system. Gandhi knows full well that people are born with different capacities, but he also knows that they are born equal in the sight of God. We all have the same divine spark, although virtually everything else may differ. How to realize that equality? Not by overlooking differences or attributing to them "high" and "low" values. The "ideal conditions" Gandhi envisioned may be a long way off, but that is no reason not to work towards it with patience and determination. Add detachment from the results, and you have the perfect recipe for right action - and success.

DAY 227

I would warn Satyagrahis that such resentment is against the spirit of Satyagraha.
– Gandhi, speech made at Madras, March 18, 1919

Gandhi's conception of nonviolence challenges us to transform resentment. This goes beyond our words and action to directly penetrate our thoughts. The upshot, and the hypothesis for nonviolence, is this: our states of mind affect the quality and impact of our words and actions. So, if you are going to try to benefit someone or some situation, don't neglect the mind. The Buddha said it beautifully twenty-five hundred years ago:

> "He cheated me; he struck me; he robbed me":
> those caught in resentful thoughts never find peace.
>
> "He insulted me, he struck me, he cheated me, he robbed me":
> those who give up resentful thoughts surely find peace.
>
> For hatred does not cease by hatred at any time: hatred ceases by love. This is an unalterable law.

DAY 228

Your difficulty is not numerical inferiority but the feeling of helplessness that has seized you and the habit of depending on others.
– Gandhi, *Mahatma 7.255*

Gandhi was accused of using the term swaraj for "freedom" because of its very deep spiritual significance. His response? Guilty as charged. He had used the word deliberately, because what he was engaged in was precisely that: a spiritual struggle that begins and ends with our independence from others. It is only when we are truly free, or independent, that we can really give. There had always been boycotts, but he asked his followers (in this case, most of India) to spin and weave their own cloth, *then* boycott British imports. It was concrete and economic, and it also symbolized individual freedom that enabled one to see beyond the illusion of helplessness and dependency that is always the first weapon of oppression.

DAY 229

Our bodies are the real temples rather than
buildings of stone.
– Gandhi, *Harijan,* January 4, 1948

Spoken a couple of weeks before Gandhi shed his body, this quote shines a spotlight on his thinking around spirituality and politics, and consequently on the essence of his nonviolence: Life is sacred, so our dealings with all of life and one another should reflect this.

We wouldn't fill a temple with polluting chemicals and violent images. Yet we pollute our bodies with unhealthy things and "entertain" our minds with violent imagery. When each of us occupies our temple within, when we act towards it with stewardship, we can become a place for healing. Ansari of Herat, a mystic from the Islamic faith, once said it this way: "Make your best endeavor to worship at the temple of the heart."

DAY 230

Truth is what the voice within tells you.
– Gandhi, *Mahatma, Vol. 3*

Truth is not what advertisers tell you - or, in a way, what anyone tells you - because for something to be really true for us, we have to experience it ourselves. For most of us ordinary mortals, we would be hard put to distinguish the voice of real intuition from the cacophony of random thoughts, most of them conditioned by outside influences (many of which do not have our best interests at heart), from the "voice within" that Gandhi talks about. But we can get better at this by practice.

Meditation (which Gandhi certainly practiced, though he didn't want to own up to it directly, lest he be put on a distant pedestal) is a tried and true method for gradually getting the famous cacophony to subside, leaving the native love and wisdom to be heard again. Along the way, we can also benefit from careful attention to feedback from our own experiences. When we have an "intuition" that turns out to be a disaster when we act it out, we can go back and ask ourselves, "What did that feel like?" There's a certain "feel" to true intuitions we can slowly learn to identify.

DAY 231

As a Satyagrahi I hold to the faith that all activity pursued with a pure heart is bound to bear fruit, whether or not such fruit is visible to us.
– Gandhi, *Satyagraha in South Africa*

Gandhi is pointing to the recognition that the most significant effect of a nonviolent act (or even thought) is produced under the surface, within the minds and hearts of all involved.

As the Gandhi biographer B.R. Nanda noted, in nonviolence you can "lose all the battles and still win the war" - the exact opposite of the effects produced by violence, where "winning" equals generating more harm. Unfortunately, this outwardly oriented culture of ours has made it difficult to appreciate the true nature of nonviolence and violence. But it shouldn't be that difficult. What Gandhi means by a "pure heart" is someone who's free from personal attachment, and able to see the wellbeing of the whole.

DAY 232

Man's nature is not essentially evil. Brute nature has been known to yield to the influence of love. You must never despair of human nature.
– Gandhi, *Harijan*, November 1938

The 1930s were not a very hopeful time in the history of world politics, yet here we have Gandhi echoing across the years with a clarion call of hope: do not despair of human nature. People may be obstinate; people may be unkind; people may be downright cruel; but that's not the whole story. People can change. They can exhibit extraordinary selflessness.

Even when facing the toughest circumstances, people may exhibit an unrelenting love that can stop pipelines and wars. This love is not a soft, sweet love. It's the kind of love that resists, and protects, and draws out the highest powers in people. In a word, that love is nonviolence.

DAY 233

Evolution of democracy is not possible if we are not prepared to hear the other side.
– Gandhi, *Mind of Mahatma Gandhi*

Gandhi did not believe that we have yet achieved true democracy. To him, democracy was much more than a vote-counting system that sorted citizens into "winners" and "losers." It was a way for people to live and work together in peace, despite differences; a way for every individual to find meaning and community (and meaning through service of the community). As he often said, democracy can never be fulfilled without a thorough commitment to nonviolence - and nonviolence can never be realized in the political sphere by any other method than true democracy of this depth.

DAY 234

Let every youth take a leaf out of my book
and make it a point to account for everything
that comes into and goes out of his pocket.
– Gandhi, *Autobiography: The Story of My Experiments With Truth*

While in England studying law, Gandhi began to keep detailed records of his expenses and income. Offering some sage advice, he encourages others to do likewise, coupled with a sense of introspection: Was this purchase necessary? What do I spend most of my money on, and why?

Gandhi's careful attention to economic necessities as a young man taught him later how to receive and accurately account for the millions of rupees that flowed through his hands for the movement. Gandhi never took a class in economics or accounting that we know of, yet his proficiency in both rivaled any Harvard MBA.

DAY 235

History, then, is a record of an interruption of the course of nature. Soul-force, being natural, is not noted in history.
– Gandhi, *Hind Swaraj, Chapter XVII*

Imagine taking a history class in a mainstream educational institution and hearing not the stories of war generals and apologies for genocides and massacres, but stories of nonviolence. When studying World War II, we would learn that the Holocaust happened, to be sure, but at the same time, we would hear the stories of people like Father Kolbe, and entire nations like Denmark, who resisted cooperating with the Nazi regime. Instead of sweeping past, or outright ignoring the likes of Alice Paul or Ella Baker, we would come to know the struggles in which they participated, including the values that guided them. What about an entire core curricular unit on Truth and Reconciliation Commissions?

What if we understand our history in the present, including these crucial developments and people (what did their movements lead to, and what can we learn from them)? Would this sort of history not facilitate the transition to a nonviolent future?

DAY 236

I am clear that whilst this machine age aims at converting men into machines, I am aiming at reinstating man-turned-machine to his original estate.
– Gandhi, *The Collected Works of Mahatma Gandhi, 62:145*

Dehumanization is the main cause and facilitator of violence. Nonviolence is the most powerful way to establish rehumanization. For it would seem, and Gandhi said this explicitly, that "Nonviolence is the law of our species." This accounts for the deep satisfaction reported by many nonviolent actors, even when they have had to suffer physical or psychological abuse.

DAY 237

Food must therefore be taken as medicine,
under proper restraint.
– Gandhi, *Ashram Observances in Action*

Gandhi was firm that food should be prepared to strengthen the body and mind for service, and it should not be taken for self-indulgence. There is already plenty of research that shows the connection between sugar intake and one's ability to concentrate and remain calm. It's also clear that much that passes for food today has little nurturing value, working unfortunately in tandem with the rise of medical needs and drugs. If our stomach hurts after eating something our bodies want to reject, we can take a pill. Why not question what we are putting into our bodies instead: whether we see for ourselves the connection between our food and our overall wellbeing. If you are on the nonviolent path and give up coffee, for example, but have not given up anger or sarcasm, what is the use? If you give up dairy but don't give up hatred, where's the power going? How each one of us works this out in our own life requires artistry and determination.

DAY 238

If light can come out of darkness, then alone can love emerge from hatred.
– Gandhi, *Mind of Mahatma Gandhi*

You would think that this truth were self-evident, that Gandhi and King ("Hate cannot overcome hate; only love can do that") would not need to insist on it. But the fact is, every step further into the abyss of destruction - the machine gun, poison gas, dynamite - was hailed by its inventor, and doubtless many others, as a step towards peace.

We cling to the belief that wrong means will bring about right ends, partly because we don't know the alternatives, partly because we have not learned to look below the surface of person and event to see the underlying forces at play, which are basically two: nonviolence and violence, aka love and hate.

DAY 239

You have to magnify your own faults a thousandfold
and shut your eyes to the faults of your neighbors.
That is the only way to real progress.
– Gandhi, *Harijan*, October 26, 1947

Just a year before his life came to an end, Gandhi was pouring out jewels of wisdom about the inward dynamics of the nonviolent attitude. But without a bit of interpretation for today's reader, his statement could be easily misunderstood.

When Gandhi suggests that we should focus on our own faults, he is not asking us to become guilt-ridden or self-deprecating - or to cause violence to ourselves in any way. He is asking us to turn the searchlight inward, and recognize that there is ample room for healthy growth inside all of us, even those of us working for social and economic transformation.

When he says that we have to refuse to see the faults of our neighbors, he does not mean exactly that. It is rather that we tend to want to change others more than we care to change ourselves. He is really saying that to help our neighbors change themselves, we need to set a good example for them, and we also have to draw out their higher nature by keeping our eyes glued to that instead of their faults.

DAY 240

Non-cooperation in an angry atmosphere
is an impossibility.
– Gandhi, *Mahatma 2*

In this puzzling observation, Gandhi lends us a reminder that our state of mind determines the significance, and effectiveness, of our actions. If we withdraw our cooperation out of anger, all we are doing is quarreling. This is not the nonviolent technique that Gandhi cited when he said that "non-cooperation with evil is as important as cooperation with good." It simply means more "evil," or alienation on the human level.

The principle is that we are against an action, not the person doing it. When we keep that distinction clear, it helps the opponent disidentify with his or her action, and in time drop it.

DAY 241

He who has a living faith in God will not do evil deeds with the name of God on his lips.
– Gandhi, *Mahatma 4*

There is so much violence being done in the name of religion that Gandhi's sentiment is more relevant today than it was even in the terrible time of the partition of the subcontinent into India and Pakistan.

Religious and moral vocabulary were perfectly natural for Gandhi in his time, but they are not always meaningful for us. So let's recast his law in more contemporary terms: Anyone who has a real feeling for principled nonviolence will not invoke nonviolence in the mistaken belief that it is just a tactic that can be used for a selfish end, much less to hurt others.

Means and ends are interconvertible; likewise with intentions and their eventual outcomes.

DAY 242

I set a high value on my experiments.
– Gandhi, *Autobiography: The Story of My Experiments With Truth*

After the Buddha attained nirvana, it is said that he asked himself what led him to reach that blessed state - what did he do, what did he eat, what was his state of mind? If we set our eyes on a goal, we have to understand that all of our activities, thoughts, and words will lead us either towards or away from it. The more we realize this, the more we see that life is a chain of cause and effect, which we can learn from and even attempt, with enough practice, to direct towards higher and higher ideals. Gandhi's life, and his life's work, shows us that we can all conduct our own life experiments with more conscious effort.

DAY 243

Every man has an equal right to the necessaries
of life even as birds and beasts have.
– Gandhi, *Young India*, March 26, 1931

An order issued by the Delhi High Court in May 2015, on the topic of bird confinement, said that "all the birds have fundamental rights to fly in the sky and all human beings have no right to keep them in small cages for the purposes of their business or otherwise." Then in 2018, the Uttarakhand High Court ruled that all members of the animal kingdom are persons. These landmark statements express the evolution of human consciousness.

Human liberation and animal liberation go hand in hand. An early philosophical argument against animal cruelty stated, quite correctly, that if we are cruel to our creatures, we will fall into cruelty towards one another. The more we understand our capacity for nonviolence, however, the more we practice bringing out our compassionate nature. In doing so, we broaden our vision to see how our actions and choices affect all of life. We also expand our capacity for creating environments that foster freedom for all lives, be they bird or human.

DAY 244

Bereavement ceases to leave us desolate when the death of our dear one only spurs us on to a more vivid consciousness of our duty.
— Gandhi, Letter to Devdas, July, 24, 1918, from *Day to Day With Gandhi (Secretary's Diary), Vol. 1*

In a magnificent letter to his son Devdas, then grieving the loss of a friend, Gandhi reveals his deep conviction about life and death. He tells his son that we are not our bodies alone, and that it is the body that undergoes a transformation upon death while the spirit does not change.

More than a consolation that we should not fear death, this is meant as an encouragement that we should remember the brevity and ephemerality of our lives, hence turn more deeply to the duties we have before us to carry out while living. Death is only victorious if it stops us from caring about one another, and acting to bring about more justice in the world. Gandhi is not suggesting that his son should not grieve but urging him to nobly channel his grief into purposeful action that honors the life of his friend.

DAY 245

The true source of rights is duty.
– Gandhi, *Mahatma, Vol. 2*

The concept stated so clearly here by Gandhi could, if taken to heart and implemented, change the face of most progressive politics.

In Gandhi's vision, the lack of self-reliance was an illusion and the demand that others supply our needs, or rights, was almost a form of violence. Whatever we may think of this vision, it almost always proves to be effective strategy. After all, those who try to dominate must first convince the dominated of their helplessness and dependency. Breaking that lie is an act of power and truth.

DAY 246

We do not want to universalize the Charkha through mass production in one place.
– Gandhi, *Harijan,* October 20, 1946

The spinning wheel, or charkha, Gandhi was firm, should not become a centralized product that makes spinners dependent on someone far away to manufacture or fix them. The spinning wheels should be built in the villages, and every spinner should learn how to repair a wheel with ease.

For Gandhi, freedom and self-reliance went hand in hand. We should aim for this standard if we want to empower ourselves along the same lines. Can the technologies and devices we choose be easily repaired, or do they require experts? Can they be manufactured locally, or do they depend on centralization? Self-sufficiency in regard to our technological reliance is in many ways one of today's greatest challenges.

DAY 247

I believe in trusting. Trust begets trust.
– Gandhi, *Young India,* June 4, 1925

Trust is so integral to who we are as human beings, that a lack of healthy trust is a form of violence. We must therefore fold a discerning trust into our personal nonviolence. Gandhi holds that we learn how to develop our capacity to trust by offering it. For example, if you are in a leadership role, give other people the opportunity to lead, even with children (give them the chance to do things for themselves, and watch how capable they are).

While the net effect produced is that we ourselves are more trusted, we trust because our security does not depend on circumstances going our way. We trust, in other words, because we are secure; and conversely, magically, we become secure by trusting others where it is reasonably safe to do so.

DAY 248

I cannot conceive of a greater loss to a man
than the loss of his self-respect...
– Gandhi, *Satyagraha in South Africa*

Gandhi goes on to say: “and it is a matter of deep satisfaction to me that the laborers have realized this fundamental principle.” This conversation took place during the later phase of the satyagraha struggle in South Africa (October 1913), when the mine owners tried to make Gandhi feel that he had misled the miners into going on strike. This primacy of self-respect and respect for others - never inflicting indignity or accepting it - was a central part of his approach to life, and his strategy. It shows up also in the second sentence, that awakening people to their dignity is a core of satyagraha. This focus of Gandhi’s seems to be behind his success with co-workers and opponents alike. No wonder the People Power movement in the Philippines termed satyagraha *alay dangal,* to offer dignity.

DAY 249

Power that comes from service faithfully rendered ennobles. Power that is sought in the name of service and can only be obtained by a majority of votes is a delusion and a snare to be avoided.

– Gandhi, *Young India*, September 11, 1924

All human beings - dare we say, all living beings - need power, a sense of control over their own choices and life, along with freedom to express their nature. Gandhi wants us to understand that the one and only path to this kind of natural fulfillment is through service. A service-based path to power, he maintains, ennobles us. But then he warns us: to think that we can grasp power through majority votes is only a semblance of what we are looking for. It won't nourish us, and even, as it seems he is suggesting, degrades us as human beings.

DAY 250

My personal religion peremptorily forbids me to hate anybody.
– Gandhi, *Young India,* August 6, 1925

When the heart is full of love, there's no room for hatred. That does not mean that there is no space to resist injustice, or to say no to someone who needs to hear it. It may well mean that we sometimes really need to struggle to overcome a downward pull towards the ultimate separating barrier of "otherness" that, when it becomes a habit, makes not only indifference but, if left unattended to, murder and genocide possible.

Anyone striving towards the highest ideals of nonviolence, therefore, will one day come across the problem of hatred - not only in the world but in themselves. It is up to each one of us to decide how and in what measure we will challenge ourselves to do something about it. Gandhi had his own method that he relates to his "personal religion." What is your approach?

DAY 251

Swaraj of a people means the sum total of
the swaraj of individuals.
– Gandhi, *Harijan*, March 25, 1939

"Person power" is a term coined by Michael N. Nagler (the same Michael who co-authored this book) to describe the vision of swaraj, or self-rule, that Gandhi propounded. Large masses of people do make an impact and can uproot dictators and change the rules of how society works. But without a deep change in individuals, we only recreate what didn't work, this time with different personnel.

DAY 252

So is the capacity for civil disobedience acquired after one has disciplined oneself in complete and voluntary obedience of the laws of the land.
– Gandhi, *Harijan*, March 17, 1946

Civil disobedience is a conscious, strategic form of non-cooperation with an unjust law, carried out in a civil and nonviolent manner. Gandhi contrasts civil disobedience with "criminal disobedience," which would mean: violent non-cooperation; undue property destruction; using non-cooperation to arouse fear, resentment, and hatred; making a rift between opposing sides wider, instead of bringing people across differences closer together.

Once we've understood what "civil" means in relation to disobedience, Gandhi reminds us of two more criteria: it is to be the fruit of self-discipline, and it requires conscious choice. In a truly democratic society, one cannot be coerced into any behavior, including obedience to laws. If one, upon reviewing the laws, finds a given law to be unjust, it becomes one's duty to resist it for the sake of conscience.

DAY 253

My nonviolence is made of stern stuff. It is firmer than the firmest metal known to the scientist.
– Gandhi, *Mahatma, Vol. 5*

In his book *Anatomy of an Illness: As Perceived by the Patient,* Norman Cousins points to the paradox that the "hard" sciences are constantly changing and medical treatments can be swept away in twenty-five years, while the "soft" humanities deal with principles that never change. Gandhi's quote above uses some extreme language to drive home the same point as Cousins. It is only when we narrow our vision to the very short term that it appears that metal is more durable than love.

DAY 254

My experience teaches me that truth can never be propagated by doing violence.
— Gandhi, *The Mind of Mahatma Gandhi*

While Gandhi was greatly inspired by the Bhagavad Gita, the Isha Upanishad, and other scriptures (including the New Testament), he would accept nothing as real unless he verified it in his personal experience. This is what gives his words authority. And it shows how nonviolence and truth are, as he said, "opposite sides of the same coin."

If we are unkind - to anyone, any creature - we misrepresent who we are. When we act with kindness, even while blocking what we perceive to be another's misstep, reality comes to life in our words and actions.

DAY 255

Cow protection is a practical application of the belief in the oneness and, therefore, the sacredness of all life.
– Gandhi, *Hindu Dharma*

A religion, it is said, is like a path through the jungle: if no one treads on it, it gets overgrown. Cow-protection in India is a classic example. Having sometimes become a fetish and at other times leading to the monstrosity of its devotees killing people of another faith because they kill cows, it was originally a powerful symbol of nonviolence, warning us to abjure violence not only against all creatures but all of creation. "Injure not the innocent cow," found in an ancient Vedic hymn, refers symbolically to the sacredness of all life.

DAY 256

But as our nonviolence was the nonviolence of the weak, the leaven did not spread. Had we adopted nonviolence as the weapon of the strong, because we realize that it was more effective than any other weapon, in fact, the mightiest force in the world, we would have made use of its full potency and not have discarded it as soon as the fight against the British was over.
– Gandhi, *Pyarelal: The Last Phase, Vol.2*

Our world would never be the same if we were to realize and sustain a large-scale nonviolence of the strong. This principled nonviolence would be adopted for its own sake, not just for a single strategic objective. Our commitment to it would go beyond the achievement of that goal: our awareness that it has virtually infinite applications would allow us to deploy it not only for conflictual circumstances but also in building constructive alternatives to our violent institutions.

Gandhi's movement came closest to realizing this kind of nonviolence, but even India was not ready to fully adopt it. We should therefore hesitate to set any limits on the constructive power of nonviolence, not to mention glibly claiming that it "doesn't work." Instead, we should aim to understand and adopt the changes that would deliver nonviolence to its fullest, world-changing expression.

DAY 257

A democrat must be utterly selfless. He must think and dream, not in terms of self or of party, but only of democracy.
– Gandhi, *Mahatma*

Would it not be safe to say that the system we have at present has produced adherents who are the opposite of Gandhi's description here? Of course, our violence-promoting culture guarantees that polarization and fighting, not conversation and decision-making, will be the way our political culture operates. Advertising, for instance, exerts a strong pressure on us not to be selfless in the least. Therefore, shielding ourselves as much as possible from advertising would make us more nonviolent, happier, and better democrats.

DAY 258

Formerly, when people wanted to fight with one another, they measured between them their bodily strength; now, it is possible to take away thousands of lives by one man working behind a gun from a hill. This is civilization.......................... This civilization is such that one has only to be patient and it will be self-destroyed.
– Gandhi, *Speeches and Writings of Mahatma Gandhi*

Gandhi believed that civilization, in its true sense, would center society on the needs and wellbeing of people, and at the pace of life: slow, deliberate. What passes for civilization today is speed, machinery, technology, and death. Gandhi warns that such a culture does need to fear external threats. Its very foundation of dehumanization and depersonalization will make it crumble from within, because of its violence and because it is based on a lie about human nature.

Since such a "civilization" helps no one (though it enriches some), it lacks endurance. The revered peace theorist Johan Galtung once predicted that the American empire would fall around the year 2020, and there are signs that this is underway. As Martin Luther King, Jr. once asked, will we move into chaos or community? It depends how early we begin to use and expand our capacity for nonviolence.

DAY 259

It is a heavy downpour of rain that drenches
the soil to fullness, likewise only a profuse shower
of love overcomes hatred.
– Gandhi, *The Collected Works of Mahatma Gandhi*

Beneath this truism lies an important, albeit overlooked fact of nonviolence: that it is a force, and like all forces, physical or "living" (as Gandhi called it), nonviolence has degrees. When people try "nonviolence" in some kind of tentative, weak form and it doesn't "work," then as Theodore Roszak once said, "they go back to violence, which hasn't worked for centuries."

We must be prepared to escalate our nonviolence, increasing its depth and purity (which may mean taking on inconvenience, risk, and suffering) when the hatred it is addressing does not yield.

DAY 260

Only one who has exhausted all efforts
may say that he can do nothing more.
– Gandhi, *Mahatma, Vol. 4*

When a problem feels too big to solve ourselves, many of us tend to resign ourselves to doing nothing. A resident of Gandhi's Wardha ashram, Bhansali, came to him to work out this same issue. According to other ashramites, Bhansali often moped, with a refrain that he was powerless to help anyone. As he was practicing silence at the time to build his internal strength, Gandhi wrote his responses down.

"Don't you like doing your little bit to lessen the surrounding misery?" Gandhi started. Bhansali replied that he still felt powerless, even if he wanted to lessen the misery. "When a thorn pierces your foot, you pull it out, don't you?" Gandhiji went on, to which Bhansali said, "Yes."

"Then if you find a thorn piercing someone else's foot, would you not help him to pull it out? If you find someone suffering from the pangs of hunger, would you not feed him?"

"I would if I could."

And so Gandhi continued, "If there was someone going through agonies and there was none to tend him, would you not sit down to do so?" "I would."

"This one act of service," Gandhi added in conclusion, "would mean service of all humanity."

The challenges of the day may seem immense and impenetrable. But let's never forget our power to face even the toughest opposition with love.

DAY 261

Satyagraha thrives on oppression till at last the oppressor is tired of it and the object of satyagraha is gained.
– Gandhi, *Mahatma, Vol. 6*

In Latin America, where there have been - and still are - many popular movements against injustice, this same principle was discovered and named *firmeza permanente,* or enduring determination. It rests on the notion that in the end, evil has no independent existence.

The Sanskrit word *sat,* which means "good," also means "real," or that which is. Human nature, no matter how distorted by conditioning, will always respond to this truth in the end. The satyagrahi can and often must, as Martin Luther King, Jr. said, "wear you down by our capacity to suffer."

DAY 262

The rays of the sun are many through refraction.
But they have the same source.
– Gandhi, *Young India*, December 3, 1925

One of the root causes of violence in our world is the belief that we are separate, material objects. We see the multiplicity but not the unity behind our diversity. Gandhi challenges us to see that we share a common source. The cultivation of this awareness brings in its wake compassion, empathy and, some even say, an abiding sense of peace that affects how we interact with others on a daily basis. This is not to say that we have all had the same experiences, only that behind our experiences resides a common core of humanity, which when perceived makes violence unthinkable.

DAY 263

Confession of an error is like a broom that sweeps away dirt and leaves the surface cleaner than before.
– Gandhi, *Harijan*, February 16, 1946

As a boy, Gandhi stole money to buy (of all things!) cigarettes. When he eventually understood that he was on the wrong path, the young Mohandas decided he would write a letter to his father to confess the ordeal. Thinking that he might be punished, Gandhi instead witnessed his father being so moved that tears of love were streaming down his cheeks. Gandhi carried this experience with him throughout his life, and one should not doubt that it influenced the way that he understood the dynamics of nonviolence, or what he called "truth-force."

Making mistakes is how we all learn and grow, yet in our society we generally consider those who commit missteps as bad people who need to be punished. Who would want to confess something that condemns us to alienation and isolation? Who is free from mistakes among us?

To pave the path towards nonviolence, we must change how we view mistakes and make it safe for people to confess to them - and to commit to not continuing to do them. If society saw mistakes as bad choices, we would help and support those who have erred, re-directing them towards better choices instead of condemning them.

DAY 264

We have to live and move and have our being in nonviolence even as Hitler does in violence.
– Gandhi, *Harijan,* July 21, 1940

In practical terms, "live and move and have our being" would mean that our education, our mass media, our economy, our judicial system, and every institution in our social order would be based on nonviolence, which today they are not. Thinking through what such alternative institutions would look like, never omitting those which directly affect our mind and our vision of reality, would be the effective remedy against the growing xenophobia and neofascism that no present method seems to provide.

DAY 265

And if we go deeply into the matter, we shall come across men in every walk of life who lead dedicated lives. No doubt these sacrificers obtain their livelihood by their work. But their livelihood is not their objective, but only a by-product of their vocation...
– Gandhi, *From Yeravda Mandir*

A meaningful life requires work for the welfare of all. Gandhi refers to such a spirit of work as a form of sacrifice, or *yajna.* In most cases, as long as what we do is not towards the destruction of life, it is not our work that changes when we offer yajna, but our state of mind.

Gandhi acknowledges that there is a certain cynicism about the possibility of people working in this spirit being a majority any time soon, given the predominant values of materialism and individualism. But he does not let it deter him from keeping his sights on the reality that, indeed, our deepest nature is good and we will find people all around us - and all around the world, for that matter - for whom their work, as he says, is "only a by-product of their vocation." We're reminded of Mother Teresa, who said that our vocation is love.

Whether we work in a movie theater, in an office tower, or on a farm, we can keep our eyes on the good in human nature, and help it emerge in ourselves and others. If we do, we can find ourselves moving beyond the worldview of separation and materialism.

DAY 266

Man does not live by bread alone.
Many prefer self-respect to food.
– Gandhi, *Young India*, February 5, 1925

Which is why some will go so far as to fast, if necessary unto death, to restore their dignity - or that of their religion or people. We forget, in some of the shouting matches that pass for "non-violent" protest today, that: you can never persuade another to accept humiliation for very long (if at all); it is entirely unnecessary to do so, because what we really need from a person can be gotten without disrespecting them; and finally, that their self-respect and dignity is intimately a part of our own. "It is a terrible, and inexorable law," James Baldwin said, "that one cannot deny the humanity of another without diminishing one's own."

DAY 267

Ahimsa must express itself through acts of service of the masses.
– Gandhi, *Mahatma, Vol. 8*

Among other ways. But it seems that today, no less than in the India still impoverished by the colonial exploitation of Gandhi's day, fiendish systems force a billion people worldwide into dire - and unnecessary - poverty. Of all forms of violence, poverty is perhaps the most subtle and destructive to the human spirit. Anything we do in terms of constructive program to alleviate such suffering will eventually come up against the perpetrators of that system and call on us to escalate from constructive program to more outright forms of resistance.

DAY 268

The German Jews will score a lasting victory over the German Gentiles in the sense that they will have converted the latter to an appreciation of human dignity.
– Gandhi, *Harijan,* November 26, 1938

Here we enter on one of Gandhi's most controversial claims, that even in the crucible of the Holocaust it would be theoretically possible for the Jews of Europe to mount, as he went on to put it, "a truly religious resistance... against the godless fury of dehumanized man." It is no unwarranted claim that it would have converted the Nazis to "an appreciation of human dignity." We know from cases like the Rosenstrasse prison demonstration of 1943 that such conversions do take place, even among the most brutally dehumanized. What Gandhi is *not* saying is that this would have happened fast enough and on a large enough scale to halt the holocaust. The "lasting victory" he speaks of is of the heart. Even that, however, should never be underappreciated.

DAY 269

The opinions I have formed and the conclusions I have arrived at are not final, I may change them tomorrow.
– Gandhi, *Mahatma, Vol. 4*

We're allowed to change. If you said something five years ago that you no longer agree with, that does not define you. What matters is how you see things now, along with what you are doing about it. If you have learned something new, something better, let it guide your actions. Let's allow each other transformation and change, no matter who we are and where we find ourselves in this theater of life.

DAY 270

Nonviolence does not signify that man must not fight against the enemy, the evil which men do, not human beings themselves.
– Gandhi, *The Collected Works of Mahatma Gandhi, Vol. 8*

On more than one occasion Gandhi added: "Imperfect ourselves, we must be tender toward others." He clarifies that unity is always the goal, and that unity with "evildoers" is attainable only when we separate the person from the deed (or even an attitude). After all, it is only when we can disassociate someone from what they are doing that they can stop doing it. Thus, we see how principle and strategy fall together.

DAY 271

I do not believe...that an individual may gain spiritually and those around him suffer.... I believe in the essential unity of man and, for that matter, of all that lives.
– Gandhi, *The Collected Works of Mahatma Gandhi, Vol. 8*

The concept of a spiritual "field" operating throughout space-time in a way similar to that of gravity, is central to a spiritually based nonviolence. Of course, we can explain a good deal of the power of nonviolence without it, but it certainly accounts for the "nonviolence effect" efficiently. And it is one of those tenets long held by the wisdom tradition, which has recently been supported by modern science.

DAY 272

I am an uncompromising opponent of violent methods even to serve the noblest of causes. Experience convinces me that permanent good can never be the outcome of untruth and violence. Even if my belief is a fond delusion, it will be admitted that it is a fascinating delusion.

– Gandhi, *Young India*, December 11, 1924

Many experiences in life may lead us to think that we don't have enough to go on to decide whether the right course is to trust the good – the optimistic interpretation of life. In such cases, isn't it better to give truth the benefit of the doubt? It is more uplifting, and whichever choice we make will turn out to be self-fulfilling to an extent. With enough accumulated experience, and enough calmness of mind to evaluate it, we are bound to discover that it is no "fond delusion" to put our trust in nonviolence.

DAY 273

Every murder or other injury, no matter for what cause, committed or inflicted on another is a crime against humanity.
– Gandhi, *Harijan*, July 20, 1925

An Army recruitment sign stands alongside a road in Petaluma, California. It depicts a young woman, probably a recent high school graduate, with these words above her: "I'm Army. I'm tough. Challenge me." As we drove past it on our way out of town recently, we countered the message with: "Ok, we challenge you to be nonviolent."

Gandhi believed that nonviolence is the "law of our being," but he was fully aware that living up to that law was challenging. Any use of violence against one another is a violation of that law, a crime against humanity in the deepest sense - for any reason. This is something to keep in mind as we hear justification after justification for the use of violent force, whether it be by police; military; between family, friends, and neighbors; and any time we hear the belief that in being violent we live up to our potential.

DAY 274

If one single Satyagrahi holds out to the end, victory is certain.
– Gandhi, *Satyagraha in South Africa*

A person dedicated to satyagraha is a satyagrahi. Gandhi reminds us that in satyagraha, or soul force, the struggle is less about numbers of resistors and more about the quality of our resistance. To that end, we may find that the act of one entirely dedicated person can be much more effective than large protests and gatherings of people who are not fully convinced of the power of nonviolence. We should take heart when Gandhi tells us that it only takes a single person. Each of us can be that person. We need not wait for, or even expect, others to stay the course with us. And yet, how courageous we must be to be willing to stand alone when it matters most.

DAY 275

I do not believe in the accepted Western form of democracy, with its universal voting for parliamentary representatives.
– Gandhi, in Louis Fischer's *A Week With Gandhi*

What did Gandhi believe in? First of all, a polity informed by the spirit of nonviolence, since only nonviolence guarantees the dignity of the individual and, as he practiced it, the ability for the individual to learn from his or her mistakes, which is diluted by parliamentary representation.

Only nonviolence, primarily in the form of civil disobedience, provides a method of redressing grievances without damaging relationships. "Even when demagogues lose elections, the hatred they have kindled still smolders," as one op-ed writer recently put it. "There are no quick fixes; we need a long-term plan."

Gandhi also believed in decentralization, which in India meant village-based societies. What it would mean in our society is not clear, but given the state into which our democracy has fallen, it could be time to take the Mahatma's ideas seriously.

DAY 276

The spinning wheel enables us to identify ourselves with chores. The millionaires imagine that money can bring them anything in the world. But it is not so.
– Gandhi, *Harijan*, October 13, 1946

Money may buy us things, but it can never buy us love. It can therefore never satisfy us. The spinning wheel for Gandhi meant meaningful work. Everyone in the movement, rich or poor, was asked to spin, and they did. It meant casting aside false status barriers in the drive towards a cooperative effort for a collective freedom.

We, too, can harness that power of love and unity in our movements by incorporating work that transcends status and education, uplifts life, and provides everyone - billionaire and fast food worker alike - with something they can do every single day. Satisfied with an ever-widening expansion of relationships, we will cease to exploit each other and the earth.

DAY 277

If each retained possession of only what he needed, no one would be in want and all would live in contentment.
– Gandhi, *From Yaravda Mandir*

This reveals part of Gandhi's unshakeable faith in (or should we say, his awareness of) the moral order of the universe. The world has been stocked, so to say, with absolutely everything we need, and could go on indefinitely without causing want, until and unless people get the idea that we have no resources within us and have to grab happiness from outside (inevitably, from others). In other words, the world is perfectly balanced for human beings who are perfectly balanced. When the latter go out of balance, so does the world - and even that has a purpose, namely to warn us to get back on track. The Greek philosophers spoke of *pleonexia,* that greed causes all the trouble.

DAY 278

Society is sustained by several services. The bhangi [scavenger] constitutes the foundation of all services.
– Gandhi, *Mahatma*

Disunity, especially prejudice or disrespect of other people, caused Gandhi personal pain. Because widows in traditional Indian society were feared and rejected, he wrote: "God created nothing finer than the Hindu widow." He of course strove with might against untouchability, perceiving correctly that India would never win freedom from outside oppression if she did not rid herself of her own internal prejudices.

Scavengers, in a country where modern toilet facilities were rare, were particularly loathed and stigmatized, and there Gandhi's resistance was most dramatic: he took up scavenging himself and insisted that his followers and fellow ashramites do the same. We might recall what Martin Luther King, Jr. was doing when he was assassinated: supporting the Memphis garbage workers' strike, whose motto was I AM A MAN (a human being). A true satyagrahi cannot stand by when anyone dehumanizes another - for that is the root of all violence.

DAY 279

Sometimes non-cooperation becomes as much a duty as cooperation.
– Gandhi, *Young India*, January 19, 1921

An expression repeated throughout the Indian spiritual tradition, *ahimsa paramo dharma*, places nonviolence as the highest dharma, or duty. It is in performing our nonviolent duties, spiritual as well as political, that we gain greater and greater freedom.

There are two sides to nonviolence: cooperation and non-cooperation. Non-cooperation tends to get all of the media attention, while the power of nonviolent cooperation is often overlooked. We do ourselves a service when we remember to appreciate how hard it can be for people to get along in a culture that has created a deep sense of separateness.

To overcome the age-old tactic of "divide and conquer," Gandhi is telling us to cooperate and resist. He reminds us that our first duty of duties is to nurture our capacity to get along with others, not excluding resisting their actions when necessary.

We can only break down the walls of separateness between us if we first non-cooperate with the insecurities, hatred, criticisms, and resentments in our own hearts. We must by all means refuse what these impulses ask of us, and even do the opposite.

DAY 280

I am used to misrepresentation all of my life.
It is the lot of every public worker.
– Gandhi, *Young India,* May 27, 1926

Gandhi offers a warning and a lesson: misrepresentation is sure to happen, especially when an ordinary human being attempts to harness the power of nonviolence in the social field. The misrepresenting can be of two kinds: those who simply do not understand what they are seeing, and those who understand that they are witnessing nonviolence and want to try to stop it.

The lesson that Gandhi teaches us is to guard ourselves from bitterness or resentment; let it go and don't get caught up in keeping a perfect image to everyone, thereby losing sight of the work ahead. No one is perfect, and public opinion will not make anyone more or less perfect - that's reserved for the inner work we all have waiting for us.

DAY 281

There is considerable force in the warning given by the Prophet against his disciples copying his fasting over and above the semi-fasts of Ramzan. "My Maker sends me food enough when I fast, not so to you," said the Prophet.

– Gandhi, *Gandhi's Health Guide*

If you put together the rules for a successful fast (not counting penitential fasts or ones taken solely for health reasons) from the various places where Gandhi discusses them, the first to often be mentioned is that you must be the right person for the job. A serious fast, especially one undertaken if need be until the death of the body, can only be done by someone with complete mastery of their desires and even the will to live. Otherwise, a fast slips from an intent of persuasion to an act of coercion, where it is likely to alienate those towards whom it is directed and ultimately backfire.

DAY 282

It is easy to see that soul force is infinitely
superior to body force.
– Gandhi, *The Mind of Mahatma Gandhi*

Is soul force really superior to body force? We would need to look at the big picture. Gandhi says that it's easy to see, but is it? When we've been taught that violence and competition are sacred, it's hard to believe that they are ineffectual - unless we suspend judgment and let ourselves stand outside of that conditioning to really look. This is the basis for finding practical, long-term solutions to our political and spiritual crises: letting nonviolence speak for itself, once we have the eyes to see it.

DAY 283

A man of faith will remain steadfast to truth even though the whole world might appear to be enveloped in falsehood.

– Gandhi, *The Mind of Mahatma Gandhi*

Might appear to be enveloped in falsehood. That's where the faith comes in. Despite all appearances, Truth can never be destroyed, and an act of truth by a single person can bring around an entire people - because it is living in all of them too.

The mass media and other influences would have us believe that we're living in a "post-truth" political environment. But Truth, "crushed to earth, will rise again," as William Cullen Bryant proclaimed. However, Truth will not rise by itself but only by the courageous witness of people of faith who are not deceived by the disheartening surface.

DAY 284

If it is allowed for some that the practice
of love is possible, it is arrogance not to allow
even the possibility of its practice in all the others.
– Gandhi, *Harijan*, September 26, 1936

While we never cling to them, there are fruits associated with a reverential and circumspect practice of nonviolence. One is the awareness that you are others and others are you. It does not come all at once, but with sustained effort it becomes integral to our consciousness.

Thich Nhat Hanh wrote his poetry collection *Call Me By My True Names* very much in this spirit: whether good or bad, what is possible for others is possible for me because I am human. Or: "Nothing human is indifferent to me," as the Roman playwright Terence said.

If we believe ourselves capable of immense love, we can have no doubt that it is possible for others. And we begin to work with opponents to bring that higher nature out in them, by allowing ourselves to mirror how they are acting and what it feels like, whether they choose harm or love. It's an amazing process and practice, to say the least. However, if we approach nonviolence as simply a tool to pick up to get what we want and then put it down at all other times, we only scratch the surface of its potential.

DAY 285

Do you believe that a coward can ever disobey
a law that he dislikes?
– Gandhi, *Hind Swaraj*

Nonviolence goes beyond idyllic notions of "being the change you wish to see in the world." It is about the courage to live for a deeper purpose. For example, Gandhi's answer to transforming injustice involves creating new and better laws and systems, including parallel institutions, the constructive side of the work called "constructive program." He also tells us to be ready to resist and disobey unjust laws, what we call "obstructive program."

This latter kind of resistance is both necessary and extremely risky. When an entire system, set up on unfair structures of justice, is willing to defend itself with imprisonment and other severe forms of violence, it takes immense inner strength to be nonviolent and withhold one's support. But does that not show the weakness and corruption of such a system? An unjust system cannot survive a sustained, strategic disobedience, and if we are willing to face the consequences, nothing can stop us from offering that.

DAY 286

Real Swaraj will come, not by the acquisition of authority by a few, but by the acquisition of the capacity by all to resist authority when it is abused. In other words, Swaraj is to be attained by educating the masses to a sense of their capacity to regulate and control authority.

– Gandhi, *Young India,* January 29, 1925

Voting alone does not guarantee a healthy democracy. It is one way the populace asserts its control over authority, at least symbolically, by letting those in power know that they've been elected and not appointed by divine right. Gandhi urges us to consider why democracy should rest on voting alone. Let's work for that day when nonviolence and civil disobedience are regarded as mandatory education for those who consider themselves to be living in democratic nations. What would it take for our nation to realize that we, the people, regulate and control the government?

DAY 287

If everyone lives by the sweat of his brow
the earth will become a paradise.
– Gandhi, *The Mind of Mahatma Gandhi*

Spiritual as he was, Gandhi felt that a yawning disconnect between human beings and our physical environment, especially the natural environment, had cut us off from our awareness of who and where we are. He literally once said that "a man who does not till the earth will not know who he is."

Throughout the world, people with different occupations tend to be regarded with varying degrees of dignity. A widespread gulf exists between those who work with their minds (regardless of what they do with them) and those who work with their hands and bodies. So two purposes would be served at once if everyone took to manual labor (setting aside for now the various economic benefits): a spiritual grounding in who we are and a healing of the divide between the laboring and the intellectual classes. There is no status hierarchy more difficult to democratize, no human division more painful, than the failure to accord all people with respect.

DAY 288

If I had the power I would stop every
sadavrata where free meals are given.
– Gandhi, *Young India,* August 13, 1925

Before we conclude that Gandhi was hard-hearted, his reasoning was that it was a form of misplaced charity. He offered an alternative: "institutions where they would give meals...to men and women who would work for them." Dignity is paramount for Gandhi, and it leads to actual solutions rather than temporary alleviations of poverty or other problems. There is a concept in the Bhagavad Gita, applied to Arjuna's refusal to engage in the battle he has lived for: *karpanya dosha,* or misplaced pity. Gandhi's thoughts here are an example of this concept, and he applied it even to Hindus who had nothing after the terrible communal riots in Bihar. Nothing, that is, except their dignity.

DAY 289

To serve one's neighbor is to serve the world.
– Gandhi, *Ashram Observances in Action*

We who wish to help the world often judge our effectiveness by quantitative criteria: how many people reached, how many bad laws blocked, etc. This is to misunderstand who we are and the nature of action. It is the *quality* of an action, meaning the state of mind in which it's performed, that really determines its effectiveness in the long-term. Of course, there's an element of humility in all this, but it would also relieve activists from a lot of anxiety about whether they're doing enough. As Mother Teresa of Calcutta (now, happily, Saint Teresa) said: "Do small things with great love."

DAY 290

My patriotism is not exclusive.
– Gandhi, *Young India,* March 4, 1924

Gandhi often said that if nonviolence were to have any value, it lies in its universal applicability: what is true for individuals is true for nations as well. He also said that those who want freedom only for themselves are no real lovers of freedom (as the British claimed to be).

It is no different with love. When we view love as a finite resource to be shared only with those who please us, usually in a small immediate circle of friends and family, we have not truly discovered love. Similarly, when we love only our nation and those who identify themselves under our flag while we wage war and other violence on other nations, we have not discovered the real meaning of love of country, or patriotism.

Gandhi saw love expand from the individual to the nation to the entire world through an "oceanic circle": the individual serves the family; the family serves the village; the village serves the nation; the nation serves the world. In other words, the nonviolent nation will love the world. It will promote generosity, reconciliation, and nonviolent resistance and build institutions to realize these ideals. This does not mean that you will not love your own country and culture. Of course you will. But you do not love or respect others any less. Contrary to the propaganda of war and violence, nonviolence is patriotism at its highest.

DAY 291

A violent man's activity is most visible, while it lasts. But it is always transitory Hitler and Mussolini on the one hand and Stalin on the other are able to show the immediate effectiveness of violence.... But the effects of Buddha's non-violent action persist and are likely to grow with age. And the more it is practiced, the more effective and inexhaustible it becomes, and ultimately the whole world stands agape and exclaims, "a miracle has happened." All miracles are due to the silent and effective working of invisible force. Nonviolence is the most invisible and the most effective.

– Gandhi, *My Nonviolence*

Gandhi makes the fascinating observation that the deeper a spiritual force is, the more invisible it is to us on the physical plane and the more powerful its operation. It is an entirely scientific model - if we only had the science to expose it to view. It is so clear from this description why we have found it so easy to believe in violence and so difficult to believe in nonviolence. We are born, as the ancient Upanishads put it, with our senses cranked outwards, showing us the transitory world and not the eternal world on which it rests. All life is a struggle to reorient our vision from the surface of negativity and destructiveness to the core, the inexhaustible source of goodness and life.

DAY 292

> To prepare for home-rule individuals must cultivate the spirit of service, renunciation, truth, nonviolence, self-restraint, patience. They must engage in constructive work in order to develop these qualities.
>
> – Gandhi, *Young India,* January 8, 1925

This is a tall order. It's very helpful for us to consider it, though, because we see so many cases of people throwing off a tyrant only to find themselves in a situation that's equally repressive, if not more so. To evaluate our means correctly, we have to be aware of the mental states behind them, as well as the tactics employed.

As Erica Chenoweth and Maria J. Stephan have concluded in their landmark study, *Why Civil Resistance Works: The Strategic Logic of Nonviolent Conflict,* nonviolent revolutions bring more democratic freedoms in their wake even when they "fail" than violent ones even when they "succeed." Why are we not surprised?

DAY 293

But I can boldly declare, and with certainty, that so long as there is even a handful of men true to their pledge, there can only be one end to the struggle, and that is victory.
— Gandhi, *Satyagraha in South Africa*

The forces that govern the outcome of human events are as real, scientific, and subject to prediction and control as the physical forces we've learned (somewhat) to harness to drive the machinery of modern existence. They are the forces of consciousness, and as such, they call for depth of access - not number of participants - to bring them into play. After a while, as we experiment with nonviolence, this does slowly become clear, but the process is faster when we have a Gandhi to point out what's happening.

DAY 294

A truthful man cannot long remain violent. He will perceive in the course of his search that he has no need to be violent...

— Gandhi, *Young India,* May 20, 1925

One of Gandhi's most inspiring characteristics was his ability to accept, even insist upon, others finding their own way to the truth. The Quran says that "there is [to be] no compulsion in matters of religion," for the very practical reason that people compelled to adopt something will always be looking for a way to get back to their real belief. Compulsion is superficial. Sometimes you cannot wait to persuade an opponent, for example a despot whom you have a narrow window of opportunity to dislodge before he does further damage. But principled nonviolence, as Gandhi understood it, always looks to the long-term - and always to the dignity, agency, and independence of the human being. Happily, in the great scheme of things, these two values are never in conflict.

DAY 295

Diversity there certainly is in the world, but it means neither inequality nor untouchability.
– Gandhi, *Mahatma, Vol. 3*

Gandhi wrote these thoughts long before diversity became a core value of the ecological movement - and long before we recognized how essential it is in the health of nature, including human nature.

Where diversity, so essential to life, becomes a source of conflict and separation is when some people (usually those who are insecure in their own identity) imprint on their minds a sense of "high" and "low" diversity, leading in the extreme to what ethnologist Irenäus Eibl-Eibesfeldt termed "pseudospeciation," the exclusion of some members of the human species. In our terminology, we call it dehumanization.

If we could all learn to appreciate diversity, rather than feel threatened by it, we would eliminate a major source of destructive conflict and be well on our way to perceiving the unity of life.

DAY 296

So long as the superstition that men should obey unjust laws exists, so long will their slavery exist. And a nonviolent resister alone can remove such a superstition.
– Gandhi, *Hind Swaraj*

In his book *The Search for a Nonviolent Future: A Promise of Peace for Ourselves, Our Families, and Our World,* Michael N. Nagler recounts the story of one of his personal heroes, Father Kolbe. Known as the Saint of Auschwitz, Kolbe was a Catholic priest and is remembered as having saved thousands of lives in that death camp. How did he do it? When ten prisoners were being chosen at random to die a slow death of starvation, Kolbe offered to die in the place of one of them, and he did.

Kolbe's act of courage resonated throughout the camp, giving people encouragement to keep living, and in Auschwitz, such an act had a very powerful effect, as it was not the miserable food or shelter that kept people alive; it was faith and the will to live.

Gandhi would say that his unique form of resistance broke through the superstition propping up the most unjust law there is - that violence must have the last say. The man whose life Kolbe spared went on to live until he was ninety-three.

DAY 297

I would ask you to forget the political aspect of the program. Political consequences of this struggle there are, but you are not to concern yourself with them. If you do, you will miss the true result, and also the political consequences.
– Gandhi, *Young India*, March 19, 1925

It is easy to forget that Gandhi, one of the most politically consequential figures of our time, did not act directly on the political level of society, or humanity. It is easy to forget that our political arrangements are secondary; they have a cause in deeper cultural, and ultimately spiritual, realities. As he went on to say, "We are endeavoring to rid Hinduism of its greatest blot," of an "age-old prejudice," and that kind of thing can be touched only superficially (and often not permanently) by laws and voting.

Young people in the climate movement today have seen their global status skyrocket. It's because they are focused not only on policy change but consciousness change: "moving the heart."

DAY 298

The more we punish, the more persistent crimes become.
– Gandhi, *Young India*, April 30, 1925

Exactly this was said by Chief Justice Herb Yazzie of the Navajo Supreme Court: "You will never have enough jail space if your purpose is to punish." If only we could grasp the simple logic, which really applies to any form of violence, legally justified or not: to punish is to demean; it is to show lack of respect and a lack of faith that the other can be reached by reason or, if not by reason, by "moving the heart," as Gandhi put it.

Restorative justice, which achieves the opposite of our present punitive system, is enormously more effective at reducing crime at a fraction of the cost, since those who are disrespected commit crimes in the vain attempt to regain their lost respect. That is why the Metta Center for Nonviolence has put forward a basic trajectory: establish restorative justice in schools (which is already happening, here and there), then in the criminal justice system, then in international relations (i.e. instead of war). And explain the logic wherever possible. There's no telling how long the arc would take to bend, but it's a plausible strategy for world peace.

DAY 299

Khadi mentality means the decentralization of the production and distribution of the necessities of life.
– Gandhi, *The Mind of Mahatma Gandhi*

Everywhere today, the progressive world is struggling to devise alternative forms of organization to the hierarchical, top-down model that has been followed by virtually every institution in the modern, corporate world. That model is vulnerable to severe abuse because of the tempting concentration of wealth and power it entails; it is also unnatural.

Life isn't organized in a top-down way, and religion was never organized that way in India (or for that matter, society in general), with its basis in seven hundred thousand villages. Nonviolence could be described as an attempt to put the individual back in the picture, and that implies decentralization. In economics it took the form of localism, the opposite and potential cure for globalization and its many ills. And so khadi, home-spun cloth, was not only a way to break the artificially created dependency of Indian villagers on the British Raj (and thus make independence of the country feasible), but an organizational model for the new world.

DAY 300

It is an unshakable faith with me that a cause suffers exactly to the extent that it is supported by violence.
– Gandhi, *Young India,* February, 1931

Here's a question that Gandhi must have had posed many times: What should a person, a movement, an institution, or a society do when we are confronted with nonviolent resistance? His answer, in brief: Be patient with obstruction. Understand why it is happening, and begin to address the root cause of the conflict. Here is Gandhi's full quote:

> It is an unshakable faith with me that a cause suffers exactly to the extent that it is supported by violence. I say this in spite of appearances to the contrary. If I kill a man who obstructs me, I may experience a sense of false security. But the security will be short-lived. For I shall not have dealt with the root cause. In due course, other men will surely rise to obstruct me. My business, therefore, is not to kill the man or men who obstruct me, but to discover the cause that impels them to obstruct me, and deal with it.

DAY 301

It has been my constant experience that much can be done if the servant actually serves and does not dictate to the people.
– Gandhi, *Satyagraha in South Africa*

Nothing could be more restorative and more challenging than Gandhi's concept - and actual practice - of servant leadership. Of course, you have to be a Gandhi to carry it out to perfection, but the idea of an operation being neither leaderless (or "horizontal," as we sometimes describe it) nor authoritarian and hierarchical would be a fascinating corrective to the ways we try to run everything today, from popular uprisings to corporations and the government. Books like *The Starfish and the Spider: The Unstoppable Power of Leaderless Organizations*, by Ori Brafman and Rod A. Beckstrom, do a very good job painting the alternative structure of successful organizations, but there is a personal, or even spiritual dimension, that is more elusive: how to offer leadership without egoism.

DAY 302

Love can never express itself by imposing suffering on others.
It can only express itself by self-suffering, by self-purification.
– Gandhi, *Mahatma, Vol. 3*

We have often had the occasion to comment on self-suffering, so we would like to land on "self-purification." People often view Gandhi as an ascetic who sought deprivation for its own sake, but this is far from the truth. He took a fierce joy in living on the bare minimum, because, among other reasons, it enabled him to feel an intense bond with the poor - he had never betrayed them or taken advantage of his privileges at their expense. Self-purification is a much greater, and far more enduring, satisfaction than whatever pleasures one gets from indulgence: it expands our consciousness.

Secondly, self-purification was basic training for satyagraha. Whatever we might be clinging to, from ice-cream to anger, will make us that much less willing and capable to undergo the privations accompanying a serious nonviolent struggle. Think of nonviolence as the Olympics of the spirit.

DAY 303

I will struggle so that I will either break the bonds or break myself in the effort.
– Gandhi, *Harijan*, February 10, 1946

Gandhi was asked all kinds of tough questions about putting nonviolence into action. Most questions came from a disbelief that nonviolence can be a real form of self-defense and protection. Along these lines, someone from the Khudai Khidmatgars, Badshah Khan's nonviolent army, had asked Gandhi: What should we do if we are not killed but tied up and forced to witness unspeakable violence? Gandhi provided this answer:

> I will struggle so that I will either break the bonds or break myself in the effort. In no case will I remain a helpless witness. When that intensity of feeling is there, God will come to your aid and somehow or other spare you the agony of being a living witness to such a deed.

In a situation of extreme violence, we have to resist with our entire lives.

DAY 304

Religion of our conception, being thus imperfect, is always subject to a process of evolution and reinterpretation.
– Gandhi, *Gandhiji's Dialogue with Christianity*

Gandhi held a radical notion about religion and humanity: If humanity is not yet perfect, and humanity created religion, then religion is not perfect yet, either. At the same time, both can evolve towards higher states of perfection, to be of benefit to a wider and wider whole. That any religion should withstand criticism was, for Gandhi, a major opportunity, if not a duty: do not throw away a religion because of its imperfections; work them out. A religion, after all, is the expression of a human desire for a vision of unity, and that vision remains far from complete.

DAY 305

My effort should never be to undermine another's faith but to make him a better follower of his own faith.
– Gandhi, *Mahatma, Vol. 2*

Gandhi tried to never insist that anyone follow his ideas but to follow their own, rigorously and honestly enough to come to a logical conclusion. His unshakeable faith was that "all roads lead to the Truth" if followed in this spirit, and the preference for persuasion over coercion in nonviolence is but an expression of that spirit.

You could be doing something that Gandhi knew with certainty was wrong, like military service, but if you didn't see its wrongness it would be hypocritical - and probably only temporary - to abandon it on anyone's say-so but your own. Just imagine how much less violence there would be, particularly based on the excuse of religion, if this precept were followed. Gandhi followed it, sometimes in ways that leave you gasping.

DAY 306

Somehow we refuse to believe in the evidence of our senses, that we could not possibly have any attachment for the body without the soul, and we have no evidence whatever that the soul perishes with the body.
– Gandhi, Letter to Meera Behn, May 4, 1933

How could we fear death or mourn the passing of others without a soul, in other words, consciousness? How could the body even be animated without a non-physical force?

The study of near-death experiences has a bit of positive evidence that the soul does not perish with the body. Whenever we get glimpses of the soul, it prompts us to venerate and protect all life, and to nourish the life-support system of the miraculous planet on which we find ourselves. For Gandhi, nonviolence was nothing less than *soulforce.*

DAY 307

Sorrow and suffering make for character if they are voluntarily borne, not if they are imposed.
– Gandhi, *Mahatma, Vol. 3*

While in London for the Second Roundtable Conference on the Freedom of India, Gandhi was asked: "Mr. Gandhi, if sorrow makes for character does it not prove that nations need war?"

"No," Gandhi politely but firmly replied. "I think that this is a false doctrine. Sorrow and suffering make for character if they are voluntarily borne, not if they are imposed."

A key dynamic in nonviolent action is actively shifting a situation in which someone feels they can impose suffering on you. Called the Law of Suffering, it dramatizes that situation for the sorrow and pain it is creating. You take that suffering on and transform it. In doing so, you hold up a mirror to the person or system imposing it, evolving the suffering into a powerful force for nonviolent change. It is not making suffering for its own sake but rerouting suffering that's already there, for the sake of awakening a (former) opponent. The resulting freedom is psychological as well as spiritual.

Perhaps one day we will come to understand this and bear witness to a nonviolent war. Gandhi mused that such a result would indeed be "brilliant for all concerned."

DAY 308

Justice should become cheap and expeditious. Today it is the luxury of the rich and the joy of the gambler.
– Gandhi, *Mahatma, Vol. 4*

Sigh. It has been a long "today." As a lawyer here, Gandhi, is citing an important example of a general rule that Socrates adduced nearly twenty-five hundred years ago: that every profession has both its particular use and its corruption. While the use differs from one profession to the next, the corruption is always the same: greed.

The purpose of healthcare, for example, is to enhance human health, not to register profits for insurance companies. Likewise the function of law, he discovered, is to "bring together parties that are riven asunder," because the supreme Law is always and everywhere the law of unity. We all benefit when this is recognized and practiced; no one really profits when justice becomes a commodity for sale, for even exploiters suffer inwardly.

DAY 309

I may deliver up my soul with the remembrance of God on my lips.
– Gandhi, *Pyarelal, Last Phase, II*

As he was assassinated, Gandhi delivered up his soul with the words *Rama Rama Rama* - the name of God he had repeated since learning it from his childhood nurse, Ramba. It was a blessing to everyone who was present, including his assassin, Nathuram Godse, and in its remembrance a blessing to all of us.

As it is said in the Bhagavad Gita, "Whatever occupies the mind at the time of death determines the destination of the dying." We need have no concern, therefore, for the Mahatma and his final moment. Let us save our concern for ourselves and the world that bred his assassination, and still breeds violence. Gandhi continues, "I shall be content to be written down as an imposter if my lips utter a word of anger or abuse against my assailant at the last moment." At present this stature is beyond the reach of any one of us; but if we absorb its inspiration and renew our dedication to make every moment count in our efforts to redeem that world, we will be no imposters either, but full realizations of all we can be.

DAY 310

Non-cooperation is a process of evolution:
it has most aptly been described as
Evolutionary Revolution.
– Gandhi, *Young India,* February 23, 1921

Gandhi understood that nonviolent non-cooperation against a State, aka civil resistance, meant a closer form of cooperation among people. Assured that such actions would not lead to disorder or chaos, he rested his faith securely in the hearts of people as well as in the principles of nonviolence. It is revolutionary. Violent non-cooperation, on the other hand, most often lacks vision, unity, and strategic thinking about what's next, not to mention that it denies people's desire for peace, which goes much deeper than their desire for vengeance and retaliation, however intense those may feel.

Whenever we non-cooperate with individuals and systems in the spirit of nonviolence, we show with our lives that another world is truly possible, and that we desire that world and are willing to withdraw our support from what is no longer working. And we become empowered in the process: the more we remain aware of our underlying unity, which is so foundational in nonviolent action, the more we can realize that we are not required to obey when misguided leaders, ideologies, and institutions try to run the show.

It's an intentional shift from unconscious passivity to conscious action. Instead of locking us into the destructive cycle of violence, it releases us and enables us to move towards unexplored frontiers of the human mind, body, and spirit.

DAY 311

The idea is that every healthy individual should labour enough for his food, and his intellectual faculties should be exercised not in order to earn a living or amass a fortune but only in the service of mankind.
– Gandhi, *Ashram Observances in Action*

Gandhi certainly had a genius for finding the simplest, humblest ways to cut through the artificial and often ego-driven complexities of industrial culture. The idea behind bread labor was a) to level the social difference between those who labored with muscle and those with brain, a fertile source of separateness, snobbery, and abuse; b) to reconnect the "brain" community with their human roots (as he elsewhere said, "one who does not till the earth will not discover who he or she is"); and c) to cultivate the all-important attitude of trusteeship that could create a safe, gentle exit from all economic exploitation.

What a pity that Gandhi, largely because of his compassion and his nonviolence, is disavowed by so many who call themselves radicals.

DAY 312

[Religion] is not a thing that is alien to us,
but which has to be evolved out of us.
— Gandhi, *Ashram Observances in Action*

By "religion," Gandhi does not mean what is gained by reading scriptures, but a "heart-awareness" of the divine in things and people - and ourselves! We are all born with this endowment, this potential, but it is the job of all of us to brush off the dust of conditioning, part inherited and part intensified by modern "civilization," that covers it. As the Bhagavad Gita says, "Just as a fire is covered by smoke and a mirror is obscured by dust. . .wisdom is hidden by selfish desire."

DAY 313

Fasting cannot be undertaken against an opponent. Fasting can be resorted to only against one's nearest and dearest, and that solely for his or her good.
– Gandhi, *Young India*, September 30th, 1926

Gandhi spoke about fasting from time to time, because it is a subtle and powerful action. When you fast - particularly with an "unlimited" fast or a "fast unto death," but even with any serious fast directed at an opponent - you withdraw from society, and such a step should not be taken lightly.

There is a fine line between coercion, where the opponent is forced by social pressure to yield unwillingly to your demands, and persuasion, where the opponent's heart has been opened by your act of voluntary suffering. When in doubt, the safe course is *not* to fast, certainly not as anything but a last resort.

DAY 314

In heartfelt prayer the worshipper's attention is concentrated on the object of worship so much that he is not conscious of anything else besides.

– Gandhi, *Ashram Observances in Action*

What Gandhi calls "heartfelt prayer" others might refer to as meditation. The classic definition of meditation comes from the ancient sage Patañjali, who described it as "stilling the thought-waves in the mind." The mind is so concentrated on its object within, in other words, it is not aware of anything else outside. Gandhi maintains that such a state of concentration requires strenuous practice, not only with others, but throughout the day. No one can make anyone practice in such a way. It has to come from a deep desire from within.

DAY 315

Power based on love is a thousand times more effective and permanent than the one derived from fear of punishment... I am fascinated by the law of love. It is the philosophers' stone for me.
– Gandhi, *Young India*, January 8, 1925

Discovering, and thoroughly testing, the power of love gave Gandhi a life of simplicity we might all envy. The love he is speaking of is a selfless concern for the welfare of others. That is the ideal. We can verify it by recognizing, as much as possible, how close our love for someone (or someones) matches this ideal. The results in terms of our own peace of mind, fulfillment, and external effects should be proportionate to that achievement.

DAY 316

Unity among the different races and the different communities belonging to different religions of India is indispensable to the birth of national life.
– Gandhi, *The Collected Works of Mahatma Gandhi, Vol. 26*

Substitute "different" aspects with "different political outlooks" and change "birth" to "rebirth," and you have a perfect description of our own need today. The advance of human evolution - and the health of our societies - are always measured in how far people have come in realizing the unity of life. Those who play on intolerance of whatever differences, for whatever purposes they think they're serving by doing so, are not only causing misery but pushing humanity backwards on the course of our evolution. On the other hand, appealing to the sense of unity, what a nonviolent actor does, is often powerful precisely because it beckons back to the path where, on one level or other, we all know we belong: the path to being one family.

DAY 317

Democracy and dependence on the military and police are incompatible.
– Gandhi, *The Mind of Mahatma Gandhi*

Inspired by Gandhi's vision of personal empowerment, a pre-school class in our local community teaches children how everyone is a peacekeeper at all times, and that we must work individually on our peacekeeping skills to become more effective at it day by day. To this extent, they are creating the microcosm of a truly democratic society. What does this look like outside of this classroom and in the "real" world?

It starts with individuals training in the tools of nonviolent conflict de-escalation: mediation, restorative justice, compassionate communication, empathy, and other nonviolent skills necessary to work out our conflicts without relying on someone else to do it for us. The moment we give away our capacity to handle conflict creatively and constructively, we invite in power abuse and violence in those who take up the job for us. It is too precious a capacity, and too instrumental to true democracy, to give away.

DAY 318

People will never be able to live in peace with each other in towns and palaces. They will then have no recourse but to resort to both violence and untruth. We can realize truth and nonviolence only in the simplicity of village life.

– Gandhi, Letter to Nehru, October, 1945

This is one of Gandhi's strongest statements on the role of villages, for which viable neighborhoods, or even apartment blocks, might be a Western equivalent, if they were to function like villages. His thought underscores the challenge we face in rebuilding a life of material simplicity and trusting relationships, which, if Gandhi is right, is pretty much a necessity if we are to avoid "violence and untruth."

DAY 319

To remove the disease, we must first find
the underlying cause. To find the remedy
will then be a comparatively easy task.
– Gandhi, *Harijan*, September 15, 1940

When tragedy happens, the mass media lure us into asking trivial questions that lead us further away from the cause. *What kind of bullet was he shot with? Where was his mother born?* Such superficial questions might boost ratings, but they do little to help us put an end to the cultural illnesses of gun and gang violence. How can we get to the root of it?

Gandhi offers us two challenges: try to understand nonviolence as a form of health, and seek the root cause of violence and address that first. The cause of violence could be a lacking sense of belonging, exacerbated by our society's unjust structures. We could also look at education systems that dehumanize us or give us a misleading sense of what it means to be a human being. Too often, there are simply no alternatives, leaving violence as the only option. The remedy is always nonviolence, broadly considered: we must change the image of who we are, cultivate radical inclusivity, and re-create our structures to reflect that humanizing image.

DAY 320

The spirit of nonviolence necessarily leads to humility.
– Gandhi, *Young India,* January 12, 1921

Humility is one of those delicate virtues that disappears the moment we think we have attained it. If Gandhi was a humble man, it was not because he lived frugally or because he wore home-spun cloth. Humility is a state of heart, a willingness to see oneself in relation to the whole, instead of using personal changes to draw attention to oneself.

Instead of working for one's own gain, or even the utilitarian notion of the "greatest good for the greatest number," the nonviolent spirit seeks to find the solution that works for everyone.

Instead of believing we have the whole truth, nonviolence requires of us to admit that we can see only part of the picture. Every individual holds one part of the truth.

Instead of changing others first, we examine our own motives and change those where needed.

Instead of thinking that we can go at it alone, we glimpse how small we really are, and with detachment, we see a power moving through us, and it affects us deeply - we are not the "doers," as Gandhi might say.

DAY 321

Some of the immediate and brilliant results of modern inventions are too maddening to resist. But I have no manner of doubt that the victory of man lies in that resistance. We are in danger of bartering away the permanent good for a momentary pleasure.

– Gandhi, *Young India*, June 2, 1927

Perhaps it is because we have no collective vision of a higher form of pleasure that we run after material goods, in the hopes of some temporary satiation of our unconscious longing for a lasting satisfaction. Maybe we do not believe - or have simply been conditioned to doubt - that it is possible to achieve a permanent good. Gandhi tells us that our salvation lies in breaking through those doubts and taking on the challenge to find out for ourselves.

He gives us an important clue: resist momentary pleasure. Let it pass as any other form of temporary agitation, like waves in the ocean. When we gain control over that agitation, the waves can subside. And we might find immense peace and inward strength - two key elements of permanent satisfaction - when we playfully and consciously resist, instead of indulge, our cravings for the latest gadget or whatever.

DAY 322

Those who say that religion has nothing to do
with politics do not know what religion means.
– Gandhi, *The Story of My Experiments with Truth*

What does Gandhi mean when he refuses to separate religion from politics? That true realization, or religion, requires concrete expression. Consider the life of José María Arizmendiarrieta, who founded the Mondragón cooperatives. As a young man, he promoted Basque identity as a journalist for a Basque newspaper. During the Spanish Civil War, he was arrested for his actions and sentenced to death by firing squad, but escaped due to an administrative oversight.

Arizmendiarrieta returned to his studies and soon thereafter became a Catholic priest. He was sent to work in a village where a priest was shot by Franco's forces and the people were suffering from the consequences of the war, including a high level of poverty and unemployment. Longing to be of service, Arizmendiarrieta realized he could dedicate his work to helping the village rebuild itself along the lines of a long-standing tradition in Basque country: the cooperative.

In 1943, he established a technical college to train people to become managers, engineers, and skilled workers for local companies. Together with five technical school graduates, he formed the now world-famous Mondragón Corporation. The year was 1956, and their first product was paraffin heaters. Today, the cooperative employs more than one hundred thousand people. His Catholic social teachings had a concrete expression - the economic uplift of a village - without which those teachings would be just nice words.

DAY 323

Individual civil disobedience among an unprepared people and by leaders not known to or trusted by them is of no avail, and mass civil disobedience is an impossibility.
– Gandhi, *Young India,* January 9, 1930

Because we are unschooled in civil disobedience, or almost any dimension of nonviolence, we often rush into actions with only superficial imitations of the models we know a bit about from the more famous campaigns.

The capacity for nonviolence is part of our evolutionary inheritance, but the practice of it in the modern world needs as much cultivation as the capacity to speak a language, though we're born with the ability to do so.

DAY 324

From my experience of hundreds, I was going to say thousands, of children I know that they have perhaps a finer sense of honor than you and I have.
– Gandhi, *Young India,* November 19, 1931

How often do our media turn to hear the voices of children when violence occurs? We may see photographs of them, but where are their voices? Unheard, they are used as tools to spark outrage and grief, which can then be used to convince us to take up arms, to increase "security" or support violent retaliation. We do this in the name of protecting the children, but is that the reality?

After a terrorist attack in Paris, one French news channel did speak with people of all ages, including a nine-year-old girl. This child spoke eloquently, saying that when she heard what had happened, she was overwhelmed and asked her mother if she would take her the next day to see the vigil. As her tears started falling, she said firmly, "I don't want there to be any war." Her worry was real, and her nobility - her humanity - was palpable. Should we not hear from children regularly?

Children do not want violence. Why do we justify it in their names? We need to learn to see them as full of dignity, and take action that upholds that dignity.

DAY 325

My aim is not to be consistent with my previous statements on a given question, but to be consistent with truth as it may present itself to me at a given moment. The result has been that I have grown from truth to truth.
– Gandhi, *Harijan*, August 30, 1939

Gandhi relied on the natural laws that govern the universe, like Truth. He dedicated his life to discovering Truth: He was not chasing after money, fame, or power. People like him remind us that to follow Truth, we must be willing to sacrifice everything for it. It's an incremental process for most of us, and one that is steadily reflected in Gandhi's life.

DAY 326

Nonviolence, being the mightiest force in the world,
and also the most elusive in its working, demands
the greatest exercise of faith.
– Gandhi, *Mahatma Vol. 5*

In the words of Augustine and later Fathers of the Church: "I believe in order to understand" (*credo ut intellegam*). This technique has been criticized as conducive to blind belief, but what it really means, and what Gandhi conveys here, is that in notable yet "elusive" subjects like nonviolence (or God), we need to suspend our conditioned disbelief provisionally to see the operation of the principle. When you have seen nonviolence succeed time and again - which presupposes you know what to look for! - your belief in the principle becomes grounded in observation and personal experience.

DAY 327

God resides in every human form, indeed in every particle of His creations, in everything that is on His earth.
– Gandhi, *Mahatma Vol. 4*

To the extent that the Western worldview recognizes the existence of a being we can call God, that being is said to have created the world more or less the way a carpenter creates a table. According to this worldview, God is apart from the world and apart from us - a concept that the mystics of all ages, including our own, refute. The Quakers, for example, speak of "that of God in every man" (every person). It is easy to see how this belief, which has always been more mainstream in India, would lead to an aversion to violence and a keen sense of human dignity, the core of ahimsa.

DAY 328

If I had no sense of humor, I should long ago
have committed suicide.
– Gandhi, *Young India,* August 18, 1921

When Gandhi arrived in Marseille on his way to the Second Roundtable Conference in London, he was wearing his traditional Indian clothing, a dhoti and shawl, which according to one biographer, "scandalized the French journalists." Gandhi's response to them was that "in their country, they wear plus-fours, but I prefer minus-fours." And when he had to go through customs and declarations, he said, "My earthly possessions consist of six spinning wheels, prison dishes, a can of goat's milk, six homespun loincloths and towels, and my reputation which cannot be worth much."

Gandhi knew he was a contentious figure. In the midst of serious times, he kept a sense of humor. It disarmed people, drawing them to him naturally. But he didn't just use humor with people who were inoffensive to him. He could also rely on it when people were unkind or disrespectful. Once, for example, when a journalist wrote a completely inaccurate article about his ideas, Gandhi said that he had a sense of humor enough to be able to let it go. He would even be willing to work with this journalist again in the future, he added.

Humor, when used gently and with discernment, can help us be more detached from our dearest ideals. This kind of detachment, paradoxically, can make our commitment to our ideals all the stronger.

DAY 329

My nonviolence demands universal love,
and you are not a small part of it.
It is that love that has prompted my appeal to you.
—"*To Every Briton,*" New Delhi, July 2, 1940
Published in Harijan, July 6, 1940

The story of nonviolence will always be the story of the people's victories, the expression of that irrepressible inner desire for freedom *with* dignity. Since Gandhi's time, we have seen a dramatic increase in nonviolent social struggles for justice. The successes of these movements and campaigns are helping us piece together a larger canon of the history of nonviolent action, upheld by actual experiments in nonviolent power.

Such historiography is essential and constructive work in the creation of a new narrative about the human image. We are not destined to conquer one another by violence and hatred; we are destined to evolve our capacity to care for and protect all living beings.

DAY 330

You may have occasion to possess or use material things,
but the secret of life lies in never missing them.
– Gandhi, *Harijan,* December 10, 1938

Here is a wonderful story about Gandhi's relationship to material things, in this case, his hand-made sandals. As he was catching a train, one of his sandals fell off and landed in the tracks. The train was pulling away, and he did not have time to jump down and pick it up. Without even a thought, Gandhi simply took off his other sandal and threw it onto the track to rejoin the lost other. That way, when someone found them, they would have a new pair of sandals to wear, avoiding turning both into junk. The sandals, while important to him, were not so important that he should grieve losing one - he was aware that his sense of security did not come from anything outside himself. Instead, he instinctively transformed the situation into an opportunity for service and self-sacrifice, and got closer to the great spirit of nonviolence within.

DAY 331

Power is of two kinds. One is obtained by the fear of punishment, and the other by arts of love.
– Gandhi, *Young India,* January 8, 1925

Kenneth Boulding, a founder of modern peace research, respectively called these two powers "threat power" and "integrative power," and (economist that he was) identified a third: "exchange power." Economic muscle can be flexed either as coercion or persuasion. Be that as it may, the present basis of mainstream policy is power through fear of punishment. It defines where we need to go: to learn and practice awakening in others the "arts of love."

DAY 332

Under certain circumstances fasting is the one weapon which God has given us for use in times of utter helplessness.... Absence of food is an indispensable but not the largest part of it. The largest part is the prayer - communion with God. It more than adequately replaces physical food.

— Gandhi, in a letter to Meera Behn, in *From Yeravda Mandir*

A story in Western spiritual lore brings us a student asking his preceptor, "Since God is all-knowing, why do we have to ask him for what we want in prayer?" The answer is, "He already knows what you want; the purpose of the prayer is to get you into the state of mind to receive it."

Likewise, Gandhi hints at a dimension of fasting that helps us get into a more concentrated and deeper state, which is itself satisfying (as he stresses here) and puts even more pure energy behind our wishes for change.

DAY 333

If one takes to Satyagraha without having measured his own strength and afterwards sustains a defeat, he not only disgraces himself but also brings the matchless weapon of Satyagraha into disrepute.

– Gandhi, *Satyagraha in South Africa*

One of the reasons it has taken so long for nonviolence to be understood, even noticed, is our failure to realize that it is a force that can be measured scientifically, that there is a right (more effective) and wrong (less effective) way to engage it. Therefore, when we meet with defeat, people blame not our relative weakness as practitioners, but the principle, or force, itself.

DAY 334

The whole world is like the human body with its various members. Pain in one member is felt in the whole body.
– Gandhi, *Harijan*, May 26, 1946

Preventing disease and healing our bodies naturally is the goal of the five-thousand-year-old practice of Ayurveda, the science (*veda*) of life (*ayur*). Its approach is to nourish the whole human being - mind, body, and spirit. Ayurvedic medicine seeks cures in the environment around us. *Perhaps try this flower growing around your house or this nut from the tree in your backyard to work on what ails you.* Ayurveda confirms that all of life is teeming with wisdom if we were trained to recognize and harness it.

Gandhi was fascinated by health, be it caring for his ill father, running an ambulance corps in the Boer War in South Africa, or attending to the wellbeing of those who came to him. He often expressed the wish to become a nurse, and his experiments in health do not fall far from the tree of nonviolent social action, for nonviolence is a preventative and curative medicine for societal malaise.

Gandhi was always a physician at heart - the relationship between nonviolence and the body, between our social and physical health, is not simply metaphorical: the same principle of the science of life is at work on both levels.

DAY 335

A burning passion coupled with absolute detachment
is the key to all success.
– Gandhi, *Harijan,* September 29,1946

When Gandhi uses the word "detachment," he does not mean a passive disinterest or cold indifference. He is pointing to an active state of conscious awareness of the unity of life. We glimpse that unity when we work to weed out selfish attachment and the tiresome obsession with the results of our actions. Thus, we recognize unity when we are detached from *ourselves.*

When we think, "How does this benefit me?" we are not detached. Yet when we think, "How does this benefit others?" we do have some measure of detachment, and our ability to use nonviolence more effectively emerges. When we couple that sense of selfless detachment with a burning passion, the apparent paradox evolves into a brilliant power. But even that, Gandhi says, is only a "key." At a deeper level, something else is at work: the light we shine reveals our innate capacity for empathy, joyful determination, and selflessness. This is the height of success.

DAY 336

All have not the same capacity. It is in the nature of things, impossible.... I would allow a man of intellect to earn more, I would not cramp his talent.
– Gandhi, *Young India*, November 26, 1931

Is this inequality? Not quite. Earning more doesn't mean being better; money is not life. We need the talents of the more gifted. But we don't need their "superiority." What checks the latter is the image of the human being as a spiritual being deeply interconnected with all of life. Any difference in capacity becomes only a greater capacity for service.

DAY 337

A starving man thinks first of satisfying his hunger before anything else.
– Gandhi, *Young India*, March 18, 1926

At the basis of the Indian Freedom Struggle was the spinning wheel, which represented independence through grassroots employment and freedom from dependence on the British to supply cloth. Gandhi worked endlessly to demonstrate the power of the spinning wheel, having students and other volunteers give lessons on how to revive spinning in villages across India.

While the spinning wheel held many virtues for Gandhi, its primary purpose was directly related to the most basic necessities: human beings must be able to feed and clothe themselves in dignity. This does not mean receiving food at the hands of a "benevolent benefactor," but righting the wrong that blocks access to meaningful, dignified work. In his view, only once a person has been given meaningful and right employment to assuage their hunger, is it appropriate to talk to them about political movements or God. The starving were not political problems to be solved but the solution. They were not in need of God, but as Jesus would say, they were God.

DAY 338

It is wrong and immoral to seek to escape
the consequences of one's acts.
– Gandhi, *Young India,* March 12, 1925

While this sentiment may sound harsh, there are two uplifting assumptions behind it. First, that the universe is not a punishing place but a teaching place. In Indian terms, the inexorable law of karma is a teaching tool (if we overeat, for example, a tummy ache is there to help us curb our appetite the next time). Second, that we are active agents, not passive victims. To take responsibility is to take control. With any restorative justice system, whether in schools or in prisons, the first step is to allow the offending person to take responsibility for what he or she has done.

DAY 339

If any action of mine claimed to be spiritual is proved to be unpractical, it must be pronounced to be a failure. I do believe that the most spiritual act is the most practical act in the true sense of the term.
– Gandhi, *Harijan,* July 1, 1939

Seeking the practical is always a path for Gandhi, and here he shows that the dichotomy between "spiritual" and "practical" many of us believe in (suffer from?) is perfectly false - just as, for him and some other visionaries, there was no distinction between the moral choice and the most effective or practical choice.

To marry the practical with the spiritual, our first task is to consider what needs a situation is presenting us with. From that discernment, we can then experiment in thought, word, and deed to create a force for harmony to bear on them.

Planting trees where they are needed is one example of the practical marrying the spiritual, but what about nonviolent resistance in a world overwhelmed by violent structures and behaviors? To be spiritual without addressing the violence in the world would be, as Gandhi would say, an utter failure, because it is simply not practical for our situation. This is why we often say that nonviolence is the bridge between spiritual development and social change.

DAY 340

Faith must be enforced by reason. The two
are not antagonistic as some think.
– Gandhi, *The Wit and Wisdom of Gandhi*

One great appeal of the Vedanta (India's collective spiritual wisdom) is the way it avoids many of our either-or dilemmas. If the role of faith is to shine a light in the darkness, the role of reason is to verify that we are not being misled. With only one or the other, we can lack confidence and, at worst, lapse into dogmatism. On a cultural level, what we're seeing here is a unity of religion and science, something modern civilization has sorely lacked.

That unity is now possible, thanks to the extraordinary science that began to unfold in the 1900s with the discovery of quantum reality, which put the spotlight back on consciousness. The harmony of "new" science and the age-old wisdom tradition has yet to be explored and appreciated as the "new story" of life and human meaning.

DAY 341

Mine is a life full of joy in the midst of incessant work.
– Gandhi, *Young India*, October 1, 1925

When Gandhi was asked why he never took a vacation, he replied that he was actually always on vacation. In other words, his mind was at peace, not because he traveled, but because he was at the service of others. Joy, he felt, was the result of living for the welfare of others, not in living for himself. And it gave him tremendous energy.

While many of us feel that rising at five o'clock in the morning is a tough challenge, Gandhi found that sleeping in was tough - he slept just four hours a night. He walked miles a day (his recommendation to others was at least ten miles, and early in the morning at that), and even young adults could not keep up with his brisk pace. If his energy did not come from sleep or vacations (though he did see much of the world), where did it come from? We can answer this question experientially, from our own attempts to rid our motives for pleasure and profit for ourselves, and focus on extending our awareness to everyone else.

DAY 342

True knowledge of religion breaks down the barriers between faith and faith.
– Gandhi, *From Yeravda Mandir*

All religions, despite any superficial differences, point to the same reality: the unity of life and its realization. As the wisdom tradition maintains, there is one truth and many paths. Unfortunately, faith is often pitted against faith, and such tension is deliberately used as a tool to divide and rule, of violent politics. There is much to be said for interfaith organizing efforts, when religions, instead of fighting one another, look at the systems of power threatened by a more spiritual orientation to the world, and cooperate to build a better world that works for everyone.

Consider the women in Liberia who in the early 1990s organized to bring a nonviolent end to Liberia's bloody civil war. What began as a movement of Christian women immediately grew when Muslim women decided they would join in too. Their interfaith organizing motto was "Does the bullet know a Christian from a Muslim?" In the past, the women said, Muslims and Christians did not work together. Side by side, they waged a courageous nonviolent struggle that succeeded in bringing an end to the civil war and getting dictator Charles Taylor out of power. They also realized their work did not end there. They went on to get the first woman president in all of Africa, Ellen Sirleaf Johnson, elected in their country, part of a systemic change towards real democracy.

DAY 343

I address this appeal to you in the hope that our
movement may even lead you. . .in the right direction,
and deflect you from the course which is bound to end
in your moral ruin in the reduction of human beings to robots.
– Gandhi, *London Tribune*, October 23, 1942

In our age, humans are not only being replaced by robots, but they are themselves made robotic by our single-minded pursuit of material wealth, perpetuated long past the day of its natural demise by our still-prevalent narrative of a mechanical, random universe in which consciousness came about late in evolution. Gandhi's movement, and its implications for the cultural narrative, are silently working to bring about that redirection.

DAY 344

The proper way to view the present outburst of violence throughout the world is to recognize that the technique of unconquerable nonviolence of the strong has not been at all fully discovered as yet.
– Gandhi, *Harijan,* June 9, 1946

The vast majority of human beings do not like being violent. Either we use violence because we've erroneously assumed that it must be our nature, or we see it as a tool and are willing to use it when we think we have to, for self-preservation and defending those who are precious to us. What do you think happens, however, when we learn another way to make ourselves and others secure, namely through the active application of nonviolence?

It turns out that most of us are willing to try it on. Nonviolence is, in the words of the old spiritual, "a way out of no way." The more we realize and understand that we do not need to use violence to meet our needs, the more the science of nonviolence can be developed.

Perhaps the most valuable work of our time is raising consciousness about how nonviolence can be put to work - not only personally and in our families, but in its strategic application to social and global concerns; to share with people that it is not passivity or inaction, but an active force which requires courage and strength.

DAY 345

Woman is more fitted than man to make explorations and take bolder actions in ahimsa.
– Gandhi, *The Mind of Mahatma Gandhi*

Certainly one can do without the gender essentialism in the twenty-first century, but that's the problem when you take quotes out of their time and context. What we have to understand is that Gandhi was working within a society and time where women were marginalized and stepped on even more than today within the social order. And within the colonial system itself, exploited nations were thought of as "effeminate." If we look even slightly closer, we see that Gandhi is bringing women out into the open by aligning them with nonviolence, and that he includes himself and his movement in that categorization. Women are powerful. That is his message and the basis for his feminism: not essentialism, but deep empowerment.

DAY 346

There would be no one to frighten you if you refuse to be afraid.
– Gandhi, *Mahatma, Vol. 2*

Because of his spiritual orientation, Gandhi was often able to reorient us, for we constitutionally look at the outer world - other people, difficult circumstances - as inhibiting us. However dire situations may be, Gandhi discovered, we are always able to control the most important thing: how we respond. This does not mean that there are not real dangers or that circumstances do not sometimes overcome us. But it does mean that when we can become deeply aware of the truth he's pointing out - and not just give it our intellectual assent - we gain a remarkable degree of agency and freedoms, including freedom from the resentment that accompanies the thought that others are dominating us.

DAY 347

The highest honor my friends can do me is to enforce in their own lives the programme that I stand for or to resist me with their utmost if they do not believe in it.

– Gandhi, *Young India,* June 12, 1924

Many people thought they were honoring Gandhi with the high spiritual title of Mahatma, or Great Soul. He, however, found it a burden, if not a cause for worry. Always interested in empowering people to enact their own freedom through nonviolence, he was concerned that too much emphasis laid on his own person might actually disempower people: one might offer praise for what he did but think they were incapable of it. Gandhi saw himself as an instrument of nonviolence. To honor or to show one's love for him, he was convinced, would be to share the principles of truth and nonviolence by which he lived, including non-cooperating with him if one felt he had erred. This is detachment at work, and perhaps ironically, the sign of a true Mahatma.

DAY 348

Whenever I see an erring man, I say to myself
I have also erred.
– Gandhi, *Young India,* February, 10, 1927

A common misperception people hold about our species is that we are irredeemable if we commit an offense, and that someone deserves to be punished when they make a mistake. In nonviolence, our goal must be to separate people from their deeds, and to fully understand that when we err, we need more support, care, and empathy to transform ourselves.

There can be no rehabilitation worth the name through alienation and punishment. If we can relate to that person, by understanding that we have also erred and made mistakes, we take one step closer to identifying with their humanity. A creative window opens onto the prospect of how we can work with and help restore that person to her or his full contribution to life by addressing their actions, not engaging in judgment and condemnation. Empathic self-reflection is the secret to the Golden Rule (treating others how we ourselves would like to be treated).

DAY 349

Ahimsa is the highest duty. Even if we cannot practice it in full, we must try to understand its spirit and refrain as far as humanly possible from violence.
– Gandhi, *Mahatma, Vol. 7*

Living in a body, as the wise sages have admitted, makes it impossible to be entirely nonviolent all the time. For water to be potable, for instance, the microbes in it must be removed. When we walk down the road, we might step on some small life form, even if we try not to. If we drive a car, or ride in one, we contribute to exploitation, whether to workers or to the planet.

We cannot impose our own practices and choices on others. Everyone draws their line in different places. Maybe one person is vegan and another is boycotting clothing not made with organic fibers, while someone else is doing both but using electronics made with conflict minerals. Should we then give up the ideal of living the nonviolent life? Gandhi says no. What we can, and must do, is increase the ahimsa in any area that we can, while striving to limit and reduce our harm. There will never be a time when we are totally nonviolent or totally violent. We are on a journey of evolution.

DAY 350

Every moment of our life should be filled with mental or physical activity but that activity should be sattvika, tending to truth.
– Gandhi, *From Yervada Mandir*

Energy drives human beings and all of life, but not all energy is the same. The Bhagavad Gita breaks it down into three *gunas*, or states: *tamas*, or inertia and passivity; *rajas*, or restless action; and *sattva*, or harmony and balance. Gandhi's vision of the nonviolent method of satyagraha, or truth-force, was a state of sattvic action - full of compassion, courage, and self-sacrifice for the sake of upholding the unity of life.

How do we recognize sattva? Imagine walking into a quiet room where a few people are quietly seated together, smiling at a newborn baby. There is power in the stillness, and there is a healing life in the baby. In that presence, a sense of the sacred pervades. You do not want to do anything to break the peace of that moment. Or we could borrow another beautiful image, from the Bhagavad Gita, in which our minds were like a flame in a windless place: unperturbed. Imagine if our lives could have that power forever. The promise, Gandhi suggests, is that we can regain that state. It is so very natural to us.

DAY 351

My presence acted as a check upon petty bickerings.
– Gandhi, *Satyagraha in South Africa*

The Yoga Sutras of Patañjali, a classic text on meditation and its beneficial effects originating from around the second century BCE, states (and we paraphrase): "In the presence of one in whom nonviolence is established, hostility drops away" (III.35). That does not mean, of course, that all we have to do to resolve a conflict is show up - or even all that Gandhi had to do. But it does mean, as Gandhi said, that there is a "living force" within us which is "invisible in its effects" but always works to bring peace to those around us, to the extent that we have, just as the sutra says, managed to establish nonviolence within us.

DAY 352

Worship or prayer is not to be performed with
the lips but with the heart.
– Gandhi, *The Mind of Mahatma Gandhi*

The hallmark of mysticism wherever it arises is its recognition of inner realities, the priority of states of mind over outward acts (though no one disputes the importance of the latter). What we call principled nonviolence actually springs from the same vision: even when persuasion has failed and we have to force others to do something or stop doing something, if it is done with a lively concern for their wellbeing there will be some kind of force behind it which we often cannot see but, he would insist, will work its effect somewhere on some level. This effect often shows up down the road, and sometimes we can infer the connection. When Rabbi Heschel said that in marching with Martin Luther King, Jr. he was "praying with his feet," he was referring to this connection between principled nonviolence and heart-prayer.

DAY 353

Satyagraha is an unmistakable mute prayer of an agonized soul.
– Gandhi, *Harijan*, February 24, 1946

We offer satyagraha because there is a great suffering that we want to heal. We suffer when we see others suffer, and we feel pain when we cause pain to others.

Sri Ramakrishna, father of the modern Vedantic movement, would tell his students a story when they asked him how they would know that they are close to samadhi. The story goes that a young man once asked his teacher this question, and the teacher tells him, "Come with me down to the river, and I'll show you." The student goes along, and the teacher takes his head under water and holds it there. (Don't try this at home, thank you.) The teacher finally lets go and the student emerges, gasping for air.

"What did you think of while you were under water?" the teacher asked. "I would have given anything for a breath of air!" said the student. "That's all I could think about." The teacher replied, "When your desire to see the Beloved is that strong, you know that the day is coming soon."

Nonviolence is springing up in pockets around the globe, in ever growing numbers and organized mass-movements. Perhaps it's a sign that, from the depths, our "mute prayers" are being answered.

DAY 354

Love is the strongest force the world possesses,
yet it is the humblest imaginable.
– Gandhi, *Nonviolence and Social Change*

In its essence, nonviolence is the practice of discovering and putting that force of love to work in ourselves and in the world, and we cannot think of a more appropriate place to begin to explore that force than in the family. What you are engaging in, though, is about more than helping your own family or helping your own children grow and develop into their own force for nonviolence in our world. You are helping the structure of family itself rediscover its purpose: to be a heart-centered space for the transmission of life-affirming and constructive values that connect all of us into one larger, massive human family. That's what makes love the world's strongest force, as Gandhi recognized.

DAY 355

Not to yield your soul to the conqueror means
that you will refuse to do that which your
conscience forbids you to do.
– Gandhi, *Harijan*, August 18, 1940

When Adel Termos went to the open-air market with his daughter in southern Beirut, he did not know that his conscience would call upon him that day to save hundreds of lives. Two suicide bombers were also at the market that day. The first bomber detonated his explosives, sending people running in every direction and leaving others wounded and dead. Amid the chaos, Termos spotted the second bomber was near enough to him that Termos could release his daughter's hand, then run and throw himself onto the bomber in an attempt to save those around him. By the time Termos pinned him to the ground, the man had already set off his bombs, and both men were killed. Yet many lives were saved because of Termos' bravery and self-sacrifice.

We can understand Termos' actions, easily, when we shift our view of who we are. *Of course* Termos made that choice. His conscience could have him do nothing else. Most of us, we are certain, would act likewise, if put in the same situation. Our hope is that the more we learn about nonviolence, and the more we seek to change our worldview and human-view, as it were, the less we would need to imagine ourselves in such dire straits. Until then, we should aim to understand why Adel Termos risked sacrificing his own life - and explain it to others so we can all recognize what human nature really is.

DAY 356

Ahimsa is one of the world's great principles,
which no power on earth can wipe out.
– Gandhi, *The Mind of Mahatma Gandhi*

The universe comprises unseen, non-physical forces. They are not abstract, non-living forces like gravity and electricity, but are the operant forces of what Gandhi called the "moral law." When Socrates, in his last address to his fellow citizens after they had condemned him to death, said, "No harm can befall a good man," he, too, was bearing witness to this active law. This moral law cannot be broken - we can only break ourselves against it. Or, of course, bring it to life in our own thoughts, words, and deeds.

DAY 357

Independence of my conception means nothing less than the realization of the "Kingdom of God" within you and on this earth.
– Gandhi, *The Mind of Mahatma Gandhi*

Gandhi was called out for using the word swaraj, which means freedom and/or self-rule, because it had a spiritual significance. He answered, in effect, "guilty as charged." He was convinced that the satyagraha struggle for the liberation of India was a sacrifice, and those who marched with him to the sea in 1930 were pilgrims. On another occasion, he said that ahimsa was nothing less than the Kingdom of God. These things were literally true for him, and true to an extent for those who followed him. That is why he never forgot, as he reminds us here, that the struggle was always going on within us while, or before, it played out in the world. He seems to have been in good company, incidentally: when Jesus said the Kingdom of God is within you (ἔντος *υμῶν*), he used a phrase that (in the Greek, anyway) means both "within you" as individuals and "among you" as a society.

DAY 358

Thus the lynching ultimately proved to be a blessing for me, that is, for the cause. It enhanced the prestige of the Indian community in South Africa, made my work easier, and the experience prepared me for the practice of Satyagraha.
– Gandhi, *My Early Life 1869-1914*

"Blowback" is a term for the "surprising" effect of (usually covert) CIA operations that backfire, such as the arming and supporting of the young Osama Bin Laden, etc. As a Gandhi biographer once observed, "People don't realize that nonviolence is the kind of thing where you can lose all the battles and go on to win the war." Should we name this often seen effect of nonviolence "blow-forward"?

Both "blows" are two sides of the scientific law that the kind of energy put into a system affects, if not determines, its result. If we could recognize this law - and that there are only two forces in the world: constructive and destructive, nonviolent and violent - we would spare ourselves and all our fellow beings much grief and suffering.

DAY 359

Fortunately for humanity nonviolence pervades human life and is observed by men without special effort. If we had not borne with one another, mankind would have been destroyed long ago. Ahimsa would thus appear to be the law of life, but we are thus far not entitled to any credit for observing it.

– Gandhi, *Ashram Observances in Action*

Gandhi often argued that we become truly human only when, and to the extent that, we are nonviolent. As human beings, our defining characteristic - our one capacity that marks us from lower orders of life - is our capacity for choice, the defining moment in which we consciously decide to engage the nonviolent capacity we've inherited and not the violent capacity we've also inherited. He is adding a critical point to the brilliant work of scientists like Frans de Waal, who have shown that animals possess ample capacity for compassion and reconciliation, an observation that until recently went ignored by scientists. Nonviolence is in our evolutionary legacy, and we can demonstrate our human ability to choose it - individually, culturally, and institutionally.

DAY 360

Man is a social being. Without inter-relation with society he cannot realize his oneness with the universe or suppress his egotism.
– Gandhi, *Young India,* March 21, 1929

Much of what Gandhi said, based on his own awareness, is being supported dramatically by science. Decades of studies show that people with vibrant social networks are significantly less likely to become ill and recover more quickly than others when they do. We say "vibrant," because recent studies indicate that the quality of these relationships matter: lots of superficial acquaintances or "fan clubs" are less helpful than a reasonable number of friends whom one cares for, trusts, and serves. We hope that science catches up before long with Gandhi's tremendous claims here as well: they help us realize our oneness with the universe and suppress our egotism.

DAY 361

Not to believe in the possibility of permanent peace is to disbelieve in the Godliness of human nature.
– Gandhi, *Truth is God*

Many people today do not believe in the godliness of human nature, even if they profess to believe in God. The besetting problem in the West has been its imagination of God as "out there," something or someone remote from ourselves and life. Add to this the commitment to materialism enshrined in everyday reality with the industrial revolution, and it has become difficult indeed to be aware of ourselves as body, mind, and spirit, and thus to even glimpse our inner capacities, of which the foremost is nonviolence.

DAY 362

The greatest tragedy is a hopeless unwillingness of the villagers to better their lot.
– Gandhi, *Harijan,* January 9, 1937

That people who have been belittled and oppressed so often internalize the message of unworthiness expressed by their oppressors is indeed a tragedy. At the same time, this does pave a way out, over which oppressors have no direct control. "All that we are is the result of what we have thought," as the Buddha said. Didn't Harriet Tubman wake up one morning thinking "I am not a slave," sparking her own freedom before she went on to become the Underground Railroad's most famous "conductor"?

DAY 363

I will not go underground. I will not go into shelter.
I will come out in the open and let the pilot see I have
not a trace of ill will against him.... The longing in our
hearts - that he will not come to harm - would reach up to
him and his eyes would be opened. If those thousands who were
done to death in Hiroshima, if they had died with that prayerful
action. . .their sacrifice would not have gone in vain.
– Gandhi, *Pyarelal, Mahatma Gandhi: The Last Phase, Vol. 2*

Gandhi was deftly answering a challenge posed by Margaret Bourke White, but often echoed since, that nonviolence would be of no use against a bomber in the sky (not to mention, today, a rocket fired thousands of miles away). Nothing can deflate nonviolence for those who are aware that it is primarily a spiritual force, and that there is spirit in every one of us. This is where nonviolence meets what Joanna Macy and others call "the Great Turning" from a materialist worldview to one that acknowledges the primacy, or at least the existence of, spirit. On another occasion, Gandhi not only said that their sacrifice would not have been in vain but that "the war would not have ended as disgracefully as it has," because it seemed to vindicate the efficacy of brute force and the irrelevance of the human spirit.

DAY 364

Just as preservation of one's own culture does not mean contempt for that of others, but requires assimilation of the best that there may be in all of the other cultures, even so should be the case with religion.
– Gandhi, *Young India*, December 6, 1928

Gandhi witnessed bloody massacres between so-called Hindus and so-called Muslims. He observed misguided attempts at converting Indians and others to so-called Christian values. He wanted to open people's eyes to the values and views of other cultures - that, he believed, would help them have more empathy and respect for one another, and become stronger allies for the nonviolent struggle.

Imagine if young people could identify religious fundamentalism and its violence without fearing *everyone* who practices the religion in question. The mass media would be less able to manipulate people into fighting against one another. We are thinking in particular of the rise of Islamophobia. The media would not have the power to skew our collective understanding of Islam, and the media would not be able to fool us into believing that hatred and violence are at the root of that faith.

DAY 365

The heart's earnest and pure desire is always fulfilled.
– Gandhi, *The Story of My Experiments with Truth*

If you had been alive during Gandhi's day and you wanted to listen to him speak, you would likely have attended one of his interfaith prayer meetings. Prayer for Gandhi was not merely a passive ritual. The nourishment he received from prayer became more important to him than food or sleep. Prayer's purpose was practical: it aimed at opening his heart so that he might become consciously aware of anything within himself impeding him from loving anyone, friend or foe, to his ability. Hence, prayer became a discipline for his vision of nonviolence.

Gandhi identified three main criteria for prayer:

1. One must pray with concentration.
2. The prayer must be selfless.
3. One must sense that the entity to whom one prays is within oneself, not anywhere outside.

When you stop to think about it, there must be a fourth criterion: service, or action. One might pray to end poverty or injustice, but without acting on it, Gandhi would say, the prayer is incomplete. Prayer's fulfillment is always the increase in our capacity for selfless service.

ACKNOWLEDGEMENTS

We are grateful to the team at the Metta Center for Nonviolence, who make our nonprofit mission possible. The Metta Center's staff, consultants, volunteers, and board members are integral to our efforts with encouraging people in all walks of life to discover their innate capacity for nonviolence. We'd especially like to thank Kimberlyn David for her efforts in helping us bring this book to you, through her editing and production savvy.

We are also very thankful for all those who donate and provide grants to the Metta Center for Nonviolence. Their financial contributions provide support for everything we do, from developing affordable online courses to consulting nonviolence activists on the frontlines.

Our work aims to inspire people to cultivate the power of nonviolence for the long-term transformation of themselves and the world, focusing on the root causes of dehumanization and ultimately all forms of violence. So we owe a big "Thank you!" to everyone reading this book, for carrying this effort forward with us.

ABOUT THE AUTHORS

Michael N. Nagler is the founder and president of the Metta Center for Nonviolence. He is also Professor Emeritus of Classics and Comparative Literature at University of California, Berkeley, where he co-founded the highly popular Peace and Conflict Studies Program. Michael is the author of *The Third Harmony: Nonviolence and the New Story of Human Nature; The Nonviolence Handbook: A Guide for Practical Action;* and *The Search for a Nonviolent Future: A Promise for Ourselves, Our Families, and Our Worlds.*

Stephanie N. Van Hook is Executive Director of the Metta Center for Nonviolence. She is also the author of *Gandhi Searches for Truth: A Practical Biography for Children* and co-host of *Nonviolence Radio,* a biweekly, hourlong program featuring news about nonviolence culture and movements around the world. In 2015, Stephanie began writing a daily column on Gandhi called "Daily Metta," working under the guidance of Michael N. Nagler and with the support of a substantial Gandhi library at the Metta Center. *Nonviolence Daily: 365 Days of Inspiration from Gandhi* is a fruit of that endeavor.

www.ingramcontent.com/pod-product-compliance
Ingram Content Group UK Ltd.
Pitfield, Milton Keynes, MK11 3LW, UK
UKHW041633190726
13854UKWH00006B/2467